MODERN NUMEROLOGY

MORRIS C. GOODMAN

Modern Numerology

by

Morris C. Goodman

1969 EDITION

Wilshire Book Company
12015 Sherman Road
No. Hollywood, California 91605

© Copyright, 1945 by Morris C. Goodman

All rights reserved

Library of Congress Catalogue Card No.: 67-31524

Manufactured in the United States of America

No portion of this book may be reprinted in any form without the written permission of the publisher, except by a reviewer who wishes to quote brief passages in connection with a review for a newspaper, magazine, or radio-television program.

PREFACE

There is a greater manifestation of interest in the occult sciences today than ever before. This may seem unusual in the space-age, but it has been expected and awaited by historians and scholars for a long time.

The Piscean Age, which began in 170 B.C., was marked by the Dark Ages and great battles, and came to a close with the end of World War II. Then the Aquarian Age of the brotherhood of man and of enlightenment began. Even now the signs are still overwhelming. Episcopal Bishop James A. Pike stirred the world with his announcement that he had communicated with his deceased son through a spiritualist medium. A total of twelve memoirs of G. I. Gurdjieff, the great occultist of the 19th and 20th centuries, appeared in a single year.

Time Magazine (December 30, 1966) reported "the spirit world is fairly crackling with activity . . ." A survey in the *World-Journal-Tribune* (January 3, 1967) indicated that there would be ten million readers of predictions in America in a year. It was termed the best "business" in 5,000 years.

As every civilization before it, ours is still seeking answers to questions which are eternal, questions which concern themselves with man's fate. The overpowering scientific achievements of our times seem to have compounded these mysteries rather than explained them. Their awesome nature has made attempts at their solutions still more imperative. Consequently we have returned to the studies of our predecessors with renewed interest. The invention of the digits preceded astrology, and gematria, the actual study of numbers, gave the first answers. First expounded by the ancient Greek philosopher, Pythagoras, the whole concept of numbers providing answers, evolved into the science of numerology.

Modern Numerology deals with today's concept of the vibratory power of numbers and brings the ancient science up to date. It is based upon observation, experience, and conclusions drawn consistently from the same set of circumstances. It is a branch of knowledge older than astrology. Its early concepts led to the beginnings of structured mathematics, a prime prerequisite for the study of the measurement and motion of the stars.

How important are numbers, really? In this computer age, you are a number. You have a social security number, men have a draft card number, adults have a bank account number. Numbers are used in commerce, science, prescriptions, recipes, on telephones, trains, buses, planes, flights. A world without numbers would be a world without form, organization, communication or progress. A questionable advantage to the absence of numbers in our time might be atomic and hydrogen science. Both of these sciences are a reality due to mathematical formulae worked out in the minds of Niels Bohr and Albert Einstein.

In numerology, all numbers above 9 are reduced to a single digit, some single digit from 1 to 9. This begins with the next higher number, 10, which, by adding its component parts, $1 + 0, = 1$. Gurdjieff referred to numerology as theosophical addition, that is, "the definition of numbers consisting of two or more digits by the sum of those digits. To people who do not understand the symbolism of numbers, this method of synthesizing numbers seems to be absolutely arbitrary and to lead nowhere. But for a man who understands the unity of everything existing and who has the key to this unity the method of theosophical addition has a profound meaning, for it resolves all diversity into fundamental laws which govern it and which are expressed in the numbers 1 to 10." (Gurd-jieff includes the cipher, 0.)

In this book, you will find the "key" clearly and simply explained. The key opens the door to the meaning of your birthdate, the significance of the cycles in your life, the meaning of your name, your purpose in life, and your past, your present, and your future.

The "key" may have been possessed by a greater percentage of the population of ancient Babylon than our world's. Following Babylonian civilization, the key was rediscovered by Pythagoras, 582 B.C. to 507 B.C., who coined the word philosophy. His tenets were that numbers set a limit to the unlimited, that numbers constitute the true nature of things, and that all concepts can be expressed in numbers. Aristotle himself rephrased the concept in *Metaphysica,* "the whole heaven is a musical scale and number,"—the original wording of the famous "Music of the Spheres."

The Bible, the Kabbalah, the *Divine Comedy,* and many serious, scholarly, and sometimes enigmatic works have been devoted in whole or in part to numbers. The Old Testament states clearly that the sacred number is known only to God:

And then shall righteous men of thy seed be left in the number which is kept secret by me.

In *Modern Numerology* there are no secrets. Read, and know all. Nor need you, the reader, be devout. You may enjoy the study of numerology.

So, believer or skeptic, read on, and find enlightenment.

M.C.G.

New York City
December 1967

CONTENTS

To

J. B.

So the potter sitting at his work,

And turning the wheel about with his feet,

Who is always anxious about his work,

And maketh all his work by number.

THE APOCRYPHA

Chapter I

THE ROOTS OF NUMEROLOGY

The seed of the concept of number is buried in the impenetrable past of pre-historic time. Only the roots of number ideology and Numerology may be traced. Inherent in the minds of our primitive ancestors lay the race experience of response to numerical vibration which time and culture have made explicit.

India was the birthplace of the ingenious mode of expressing all numbers by means of ten symbols. Each of these symbols has an absolute value of its own and, in addition, each number has a relative value based on its position.

The ten symbols and the universal use of the decimal system give testimony to the ancient aphorism: Man is the measure of all things. For it is incontrovertible that finger-counting, on his ten fingers, was man's first arithmetic.

The systematic use of written numbers goes back to the ancient Sumerians, the Egyptians, and the Chinese. The Chinese arranged numbers on the *Lo Chou* or Holy Board. They considered that odd numbers connoted day, white, heat, fire, and sun. Even numbers were believed to signify night, black, cold, matter, water, and earth. They incorporated into their culture the Phœnician alphabet, and its sounds and letters as well.

In the course of the development of number concept, India, womb of culture, was once more the place of origin of algebra and the system of giving evaluation to a number according to its position. Prior to the latter discovery the abacus, or counting board, was used. Children today still use these boards with their wires and wooden beads as toys or tools of learning. The abacus permitted the concept of, for example, number 6 to be used alone, as 6, as well as in 60, 160, and so on, having a different value in each position. The word *abacus* derives from the Semitic *abac,* meaning dust, or its Greek equivalent, *abax,* meaning slab. The use of finger marks to tally on smooth sand was probably the first counting system.

The tenth symbol, zero, also had its origin in India. The Hindu word for *blank* was used to indicate this concept. Then the Arabs used their synonym meaning *empty,* the *cifr.* When this idea travelled to Italy, the Latinized version, *zephirium* (nothing) was used until it was Italianated into the vulgate, *zero.* In North Europe, the Germans converted the original Arab word into *cifra,* about the thirteenth century, and and the English into *cipher.*

Gematria was the earliest form of mystic connotation of numbers. Gematria ascribed to every letter two values: one of sound, one of number. Modern Numerology follows this same pattern today, which was known to the writers of the Bible. An example of Gematria in the Old Testament is Abraham's driving out 318 slaves and thus rescuing Eliasar. The numerical value of the Hebrew word Eliasar is equal to 318.

In Greek the numerical equivalent of the name of the great hero Achilles is 1276, which made him superior to Patroclus, equal to number value 87, and Hector, number value 1225.

Gematria continued as a mystic language through

Christian theology. To the Beast of the Revelation was ascribed the number 666. Conflict raged over the interpretation of this number for decades. A writer named Peter Bungus, in a lengthy volume on Numerology, ascribed number 666 to Martin Luther. In his reply, Martin Luther, also a student of Gematria, ascribed the number 666 to the length of duration of the regime of the Popes.

The landmark in the history of Numerology is Pythagoras, Sixth Century B. C. philosopher, mystic, astronomer, astrologer, and numerologist. The genesis of his mystic philosophy is still a moot question and a matter of controversy. About all that is definitely known is that he visited Egypt where he studied the mysteries to attain purification in order to escape the "wheel of birth." Whatever the scource, he left a profound influence on Plato, Aristotle, and both Greek and modern thought.

The basic idea of Pythagorean philosophy was that man could grasp the nature of the universe only through number and form. The four elements: fire, water, air and earth, comprised the holy fourfoldness, or tetraktys, to which Pythagorians addressed their prayer:

"Bless us, divine number, thou who generatest gods and men! O holy, holy tetraktys, thou that containest the root and the source of eternally flowing creation! For the divine number begins with the profound, pure unity until it comes to the holy four; then it begets the mother of all, the all-comprising, the all-abounding, the first-born, the never-swerving, the never-tiring holy ten, the keyholder of all."

The discoveries of the Pythagoreans were numerous. They postulated the ten fundamental oppositions: odd and even, limit and unlimited, one and many, right and left, male and female, rest and motion, straight and curved, light and darkness, good and evil, square and oblong. It was their contention that the universe is the realization of these opposites.

The dependence of intervals on certain ratios of lengths of string at the same tension was another discovery of Pythagoras. Thus, 2:1 gives the octave; 3:2 the fifth, and 4:3 the fourth. This led to the idea that all things are numbers. The Pythagoreans supposed the elements of numbers to be the elements of all things and heaven to be a musical scale and a number.

The nature and quality of numbers was also a subject of study in the school of Pythagoras. Even numbers were considered soluble (which they are), and consequently ephemeral, feminine, and pertaining to the earthly. Odd numbers, being indissoluble, are masculine, and of a celestial nature.

Each number was identified with a human attribute: 1 with reason, being unchangeable; 2 with opinion; 4 with justice, forming the perfect square and being the product of equals (2 times 2); 5 with marriage, being the union of the first feminine and the first masculine number.

The greatest disciple of Pythagoras was Philolaus. He reaffirmed all the principles of the school, and he summed up his creed in the following statement: "All things which can be known have number, for it is not possible that without number anything can be either conceived or known."

Nicomachus, who followed the teachings of the school and founded the philosophy which succeeded in time, bore testimony to the belief in the mystic connotations of Numerology. This concept is pithily stated in his own words: "All things that have been arranged by nature according to a workman-like plan appear, both individually and as a whole, as singled out and set in order by Foreknowledge and Reason, which created all according to number, conceivable to mind only and therefore wholly unmaterial; yet real, indeed, the really real, the eternal."

From these early days when Numerology was taking root until the present time, a whole tradition has grown up regarding the interpretation of numbers. For their historic interest, some examples of the ancient connotations of numbers are given here. (The modern interpretations follow in the next chapter.)

Number 1. According to all occult interpretations, this number is the symbol of the cosmos, or of the diety; that it would take an infinite number of steps to evaluate this ratio only lends power to this occult interpretation, for the infinite, too, is an atribute of God.

Number 2. A material principle, according to Pythagoras. The second day of the second month of the year was sacred to Pluto, and hence esteemed unfortunate.

Number 3. A perfect number, according to the ancients, expressive of beginning, middle, and end. Mythology ascribed the rule of the world to three gods: Jupiter (heaven), Neptune (sea), and Pluto (Hades). Jove holds the three-forked lightning, Neptune the trident, and Pluto the three-headed dog.

Number 4. The number of letters in the word *Lord,* for God, is the same in countless ancient and modern languages. For example, there are four letters for this word in *Deus,* Latin; *Dieu,* French; *Adat,* Assyrian; *Godt,* Dutch; *Gott,* German; *Godh,* Danish; *Soru,* Persian; and so on, in Greek, Hebrew, Swedish, Cabalistic, Egyptian, Sanskrit, and many others for which words the characters do not exist in English print shops.

Number 5. This is the pentad, or great mystic number, because it is the sum of adding two, the first even, and three, the first odd number, together. All the powers of nature are contained herein since 1 is unity, 2 diversity, 3 their compound, hence — 5, all the principles in operation.

Number 6. "Six is a perfect number in itself, and not because God created all things in six days; rather the inverse is true; God created all things in six days because this number is perfect, and it would remain perfect even if the work of the six days did not exist." — St. Augustine.

Number 7. This was considered a holy number, for there are seven days in creation, seven days in the week, and seven phases of the Moon. In the Bible, Pharaoh saw seven kine and seven ears of corn in his dream, and also "For seven days seven priests with seven trumpets invested Jericho, and on the seventh day they encompassed the city seven times."

Number 8. The number of the beatitudes in the Book of Matthew. It is also the symbol of the sign of opposition.

Number 9. A mystical number, being thrice three, hence the perfect plural. It represents perfection or completion.

And so we end the investigation of the roots of

Numerology with the number of completion, and the immortal words of Pythagoras. "Number rules the Universe."

NUMERALS OF ANCIENT TIMES

Hindu Numerals, found in a cave in India, and dating from the Second or Third Century, B. C.

Hindu Numerals, about a thousand years old. They found their way to Europe via Baghdad.

Arabic Numerals, from which the present forms descended. The Persian Numerals were the same.

Arabic Numerals, from which the present form was adopted. They are written backwards, right to left.

Chapter II

THE NATURE OF NUMBERS

A number is the name of a hidden law. Whether you try to trace the historical background of numbers or accept the Biblical story of Creation, number enters as a vital element. "In the beginning" stands for number 1, the first day. "And on the seventh day, He rested." Number 7 symbolized the closing of a cycle, and still does. In these two numbers, then, are represented the Law of Creation and the Law of Culture.

In this book, all the cycles and letters are fully explained. Thus, the reader has all the meanings and implications of the effect of numbers pre-digested and simply expressed for his use and guidance. However, for those readers who wish to make studies of cycles and names by themselves, or merely out of intellectual curiosity desire to know it, the nature of each number is presented here.

Number 1 is symbolic of man standing upright. The word *man* works out to this number, thus:

$$
\begin{array}{ccc}
1 & = & 1 \\
m \quad a \quad n & & \\
4 \qquad 5 & = & 9 \\
\hline
& & 10 \\
1 + 0 & = & 1
\end{array}
$$

The nature of the number 1 is intellectual and masculine. It denotes change and pioneering work. New events, new conditions, and travel are indicated when

the number 1 appears in a name or cycle. Will power
is so developed in a 1 cycle that it can establish its
goal, and it usually has a definite purpose for its actions. When not used for the achievement of its goal,
the nature of the 1 changes, and it becomes domineering, ruthless, selfish, and makes its new aim self-grati-
fication, rationalizing its acts as "duty."

The planetary equivalent of the number 1 is the
Sun, symbolic of life-giving days, creation, vitality, new
beginnings, intellectual qualities, inventiveness, genius, originality, and brilliance.

Number 2 symbolizes building into form. It is
the second deliberate act (after creation). It is feminine in nature, and so represents woman. It is emotional and intuitive. The number 2 builds with the materials at hand, and so represents the law of cooperation.
It is slow in nature, and warm in temperament. This
number in a name stands for the ability to develop tact
and diplomacy; in a cycle, it represents the requirement to cooperate. When not correctly used, its force
turns to timidity, deceit, and secrecy.

The planetary equivalent of the number 2 is the
Moon, symbolic of woman, domesticity, helpfulness,
cycles, instability, and deliberation.

Number 3 represents the law of love and affection.
It deals with people, and reigns over family life and
social contacts. This is the number of expression; it
brings both the intellect and the intuition to play in
the various fields of art. It is a joyful number, giving
the opportunity for play and entertainment. It is
both hopeful and wishful in temperament. The number
3 in a name represents popularity; in a cycle, it represents destiny, be it success or failure — as you use its

vibratory power. The 3 is the number of the child, marriage, and intrigue. When its force is used for ethical ends, it spells achievement; when not so used, it denotes carelessness, a happy-go-lucky attitude, and the scattering of one's talents.

The planetary equivalent of the number 3 is Jupiter, symbolic of good fortune, success, fame, material comforts, and happiness.

Number 4 is the number of hard work. It connotes the building of a firm foundation. It endows the power to organize and to work in organizations. It is cold, intellectual, and slow in its nature. In a name, it represents discipline, in a cycle, it represents restriction — the restriction brought about by the need to work hard. It is symbolized by the square from which one can work one's way out, or rise above it. The number 4 represents the law of justice without mercy, tolerance, or sympathy.

The planetary equivalent of the number 4 is Saturn, symbolic of the taskmaster, the time-keeper, the teacher, the "brake" that slows down aspirations and returns one to reality.

Number 5 symbolizes the law of gathering new experiences. It denotes change, travel, new friends, and it is detached from everything. It connotes an interest in religion and in religious institutions. It is rapid in nature, careless in action, and speculative in temperament; above all, it demands freedom of action. In its domain are salesmanship, research, and talk. It seeks present happiness, and cares little for the cost or consequence.

The planetary equivalent of number 5 is Mercury, symbolic of speed, communications, changeability, temperament, writing, talking, travel, contracts, and radio.

Number 6 symbolizes the law of material supply. It brings money to those who make an effort. It is the law of education, and it also governs married life. Harmony in the home and community result from its vibratory force. It deals with large groups and institutions. Its aim is to establish beauty, harmony, and rhythm. In a name or cycle, it denotes the need to assume a responsibility other than one's own. It represents a blend of the intellectual and emotional. It can never let the influence feed on bread alone, but requires happiness through cultural pursuits.

The planetary equivalent of number 6 is Venus, which represents beauty, harmony, rhythm, art, balance, the drama, family life, and happiness as its expression.

Number 7 symbolizes the law of culture. It is cold and intellectual in nature. It is the number which has in its domain the control of inventors, musicians, and composers. It deals with the home, and the responsibilities of the household. Under its influence are atmospheric conditions, health, good conduct, and philosophical studies. It is slow and subtle in its effect. When its vibratory force is not used constructively, it denotes quiet, deceit, and stubbornness.

The planetary equivalent of the number 7 is Uranus, which denotes willful action of an unexpected nature, surprising changes, and forces that can be pre-predicted only by deep study.

Number 8 symbolizes justice with mercy. It is the number of power, and denotes wealth to him who comes under its vibratory force. It also denotes the doing of good deeds, and sharing the material treasures that it awards. It is cold and masculine in nature, and it denotes good health, energy, and endurance. Discipline and discrimination are the lessons learned by those whose names are marked by this number or who enter a cycle under its influence. The power it endows is to be used for the improvement of mankind, and if it is diverted to other uses, it brings destruction, in the end destroying itself.

The planetary equivalent of the number 8 is Mars, denoting unrestrained and unleashed power which must be harnessed for good purposes to be kept from destroying all that comes within its reach.

Number 9 denotes the law of Karma. It deals with the occult, with philosophy, and with cultural development. It governs the fine arts which do not come under the rulership of number 6. This is the number which puts one through life's tests. It establishes the balance of material, spiritual, and bodily things. It gives, and it takes away — according to the deserts of the one under its influence. Everything is paid for by a person whose name is strongly studded with 9's or who is under the influence of the 9 in a cycle. It is the most humanitarian of numbers, and should be treated with great respect.

The planetary equivalent of the number 9 is Neptune, symbolizing the occult, the mysterious, and the hidden factors in heaven and on earth.

The Zero, O, represents limited space in which the intellectual principle creates. It represents the greater strength; after a number, it increases that number's strength by 10, and so on, for as many times as it is repeated.

The planetary equivalent is Pluto, whose discovery was so recent that its powers are hardly known. It is said to represent the forces of the world of darkness, but further research and study are required before a definite statement can be made.

Chapter III
YOUR LIFE CYCLE

Added together, the digits in your date of birth comprise your number of destiny. Your birthday is not an "accident," but part of the Great Plan of the Creator. Behind the numbers in your date of birth is an occult significance which has a bearing upon your entire life.

This number of destiny is your Life Cycle Number, which you may quickly compute by following the directions given immediately below.

To Compute Your Life Cycle Number

To compute your Life Cycle Number, add together the number value of your month, day, and year of birth.

The number value of each month is:

January	1	July	7
February	2	August	8
March	3	September	9
April	4	October	1
May	5	November	2
June	6	December	3

1) Take the number value of the month you were born, and add to it the number of the day and the year you were born.

For example, if you were born on January 19, 1909, you would add,

24

January .... number value   1
Date 19
Year 1909
                    Total 1929

   2)   Reduce this total to a single digit,
1 plus 9 plus 2 plus 9 equal 21,
2 plus 1 equal 3.

   Thus, the number of this person's Life Cycle or
number of destiny, is 3.

   Your Life Cycle represents the trends and tendencies of your whole existence and the work you are here
to do. It denotes the role you are to play in the Cosmic
Drama, and gives you the clue to your destiny.

   Your moral strength, your innate characteristics,
and your predominating states of mind are revealed in
the Life Cycle Number. Your true self is comprised of
the latent powers of your character and is revealed by
the strength of your purpose in life.

   From birth to the end of life, you will express the
power conferred upon you by this number of destiny.
The consciousness of your cosmic heritage is expressed
in this number, for no matter how often you change
your name and consequently its expression, you can
never change your birthday.

   Your birth-right, as interpreted from the number
of your Life Cycle, is given in the divisions which
follow.

No. I Life Cycle
"THE PIONEER"

   You are the Pioneer, the leader, the captain, and
the planner. Yours is a very positive nature, for you
have a truly strong individuality. Your place in the

path of life is in the driver's seat of the chariot of experience. Servitude is unknown to you, and subservience is completely alien to your nature.

You are original and creative and possess the aggressive qualities necessary to put your productive ideas into practical, material form. Ambition is a prime factor in your life, and it motivates you to strive arduously for the success you desire. You are endowed with executive ability, and can direct affairs, whether they be those of a large organization or the household.

Determination, strength, and will are the tools of your ambition, and you use them with the authority of one who has skill and training.

Occassionally you demonstrate the negative aspects of these qualities. At such times you are domineering and hasty. It is wiser for you to use diplomacy and get your way than to try to impose it on others by sheer force of will.

You are inclined to be critical and demanding, but somewhat unable to take criticisms others offer to you, for deep within your nature is a sensitivity you try to conceal.

Follow the generous impulses of your heart, and you will retain your leadership and your friendships.

No. 2 Life Cycle
"The Helpmate"

You can acquire what you want without fanfare, for tact and diplomacy have been endowed upon you as two distinguishing characteristics. The keynote of your life is cooperation; you succeed more mightily by carrying out the plans of others, by executing the blue-print or pattern that is designed rather than by attempting to be completely original in your own sphere.

Disharmony and disagreeable situations take a toll upon your nervous system, and for this reason, you do all within your power to establish and maintain harmony. You have natural grace and great consideration for others — two traits which win you a host of friends.

While you lack the aggressive spirit of those born with other numbers of destiny, this does not mean that you need ever lack the good things of life. Two is the number of "gathering in." Your own cooperative spirit inflates your powers of association, and brings to you many things that others go forth to seek. Rhythm is the one requirement for your happiness.

At your best, you display the wonderful traits of agreeability, charm, and courtesy. The symbol of your number of destiny is the soul being breathed into the body. In other words, your function is to fill the empty forms with life. There is a kind of magic connected with all you do, for you seem to take the concept and kindle true life into it. Whereas others seek the company and assistance of their fellows, you have an unusual independence of spirit that makes you the perfect helpmate, yet completely self-sufficient if you need to be so.

The hammer can not get along without the forge, and you are the hard metal on which the shape eternal is formed.

No. 3 Life Cycle
"THE ARTIST"

You are the pinnacle of self-expression. Mentality plays a very large part in your life, for you see clearly and wholly. No delusions waste your time, even though you are pleasure-loving. You realize that all life is not mere fun.

Versatality is one of your outstanding traits. You have so many talents that you have dificulty in choosing a single one to express all that is within you, waiting to come out. You are a "quick study," being able to acquire knowledge without making a strenuous effort. Your scholarship is not profound, however, for you do not devote all your time to study as the real scholar does.

You are sociable and entertaining. These qualities make it simple for you to make friends quickly. Most people like you; the exceptions are those who do not understand you. The reason is that they can not see the depth of your character, and think that your surface is the real you. Your enthusiasms are contagious, but your taste palls quickly, and then you seek the new.

You are inclined to accept things as they are, and not to worry too much. You like getting your own way and indulging your own desires. Your quick wit makes you a cutting critic of other people and their opinions. In fact, your gift of words might well make you an excellent critic or writer, as well as teacher, lecturer, or entertainer.

Love is a necessity to you. Unless you are sharing a real emotional experience with someone who takes you seriously, you are not really happy.

No. 4 Iife Cycle
"THE MASON"

The number of your Life Cycle is symbolized by the square. This stands for justice and equality, and it represents you in the center, bounded on each side, and thus restricted so that you can not expand. Consequently, the only direction in which you can grow is — up! The square represents the practical aspects of life, upon which all form is built. For this reason, you may look upon this Life Cycle as the building of foundations for better things to come.

You may look to this life as one of work. You are prepared for this by having been endowed with patience, endeavor, and the desire to render practical service. Method and logic are the mental tools which you, as the mason use. You are imbued with faithfulness and loyalty, although you are not particularly demonstrative about your emotions.

Conservatism may restrict you ideologically. Details and duties seem to overshadow the end-all aim of some of your endeavors. In some things it is wiser to go with the tide rather than try to direct its course. By avoiding the tendency to force your ideas on others, you can avoid the friction that retards your progress.

Your finest expression comes from your sense of form and design. You can visualize, in its completed form, the concept offered you by the artist or architect. Then, in your own practical way, you can execute this design or blue-print.

It could never be said of you that you shirk your duties or avoid your responsibilities. Where dependability is wanted, you fill the bill — and you do a noble and creative job.

No. 5 Life Cycle
"THE SCRIBE"

You are mercurial by nature, full of wit, dash, enthusiasm, and energy. Life to you is a dashing and bold adventure, which you can well take in your stride because all of its ceaseless change is in perfect harmony with your own love of variety. You thoroughly enjoy the activities of the world, and are the center of interest and attraction in the crowd.

Freedom is your birth-right, and you do not allow anything to interfere with your right to enjoy it. Your pursuit of happiness is an endless trail of good humor, wit, and pleasure. Not that you do not have your serious moments, for you are highly intellectual, and are a master in the use of words. As a matter of fact, the use of words is your natural metier. You could excel in any profession or vocation where a good vocabulary and oratory or vocal powers are needed. The ministry, teaching, and lecturing are excellent fields for your endeavor. In the world of entertainment or writing, you could shine as a brilliant star.

Your great versatility with language could be a cause of occasional difficulty or embarrassment, for it tempts you to talk about topics with which you are not thoroughly familiar, or to launch a tirade of wit against those less able with the rapier of sarcasm or humor than you are.

A certain inconsistency is also the expression of your mercurial temper. There is a way to take advantage of this quality, and that is to follow the precept of Ralph Waldo Emerson, who said that every intellectual person is inconsistent. He meant that the wise man changes with the times, and progresses and advances as all nature and civilization do. This is the path you may easily follow, and it leads to happiness, full expression of the personality, and your success.

No. 6 Life Cycle
"The Teacher"

You have noble ideals and high aspirations for their fulfillment. Love is the ruler of your universe, and it is your role in life to teach this philosophy — among other things — to the rest of the world. Your aim is to help others, mainly by establishing and maintaining justice and the rights of humanity.

Beauty and harmony are as necessary to you as the very breath of life. You must have these two in your environment, and particularly in your home. Domestic felicity is your immediate goal; and after you have established it there, you wish to expand the same harmonious atmosphere to all the rest of your surroundings, and the universe. The crash, the tawdry, and the vulgar are upsetting to the balance and rhythm that are such a deep part of your inmost being.

You have a deep appreciation of the arts and music. You express this love for the finer things of life either by being creative in these fields, or by being the keenest of connoisseurs.

The unselfishness which distinguishes you makes you the counsellor of the young, the confidant of the old, and the teacher of the world. Rarely critical, you prefer to instill your noble concepts through understanding and sympathy.

A certain amount of unwanted responsibility accompanies the life path of those born under the vibration of your Life Cycle. You have duties which are real burdens, but you soon learn that even these heavy tasks have their function in life — be it only to further instill in you the unselfishness and generosity that you need for your work in life.

By fulfilling your function in life, you can find the sheer happiness that is known only to great humanitarians.

No. 7 Life Cycle
"THE MYSTIC"

You are contemplative and analytical by nature. Of a very thoughtful turn of mind, you seek to discover the reason behind everything, not being satisfied to accept anything at its surface value. Your meditations and analyses should lead to the discovery of truths both ancient and new, especially along mystic and occult lines of thought.

Your part in the cosmic drama is that of the healer. To you, the troubled in mind and body turn for comfort, consolation, and healing, for your touch — both physical and spiritual — is like the curative "laying upon of hands" of the Holy Book.

A reserved manner sets you apart from other people, and it takes a type who understands the subtler things of life to completely comprehend your quiet moods. You are cloaked in natural dignity, and, regardless of your station or vocation in life, you are respected wherever you appear. Your manner is intellectual, and your main interests are along cultural and philosophical lines. Musical composition and invention are fields wherein your originality should be prosperously creative.

The lovely things of life are as necessary to you as the air by which you live. Without the fine creations of the world's artists for you to appreciate, you would feel that life was entirely too humdrum an existence to bother living. As a connoisseur of each stitch in the tapestry of artistic creation, you make each moment vibrant with appreciation.

There are many, and difficult, lessons for you to learn, for it seems to you at times that life is just one delay and disappointment after the other. It is your philosophical outlook, and your sympathy with mysticism that makes you understand that the pace of living is in itself one of the prime and most important of all lessons.

No. 8 Life Cycle
"THE GLEANER"

The harvest of study, organizational ability, and the qualities of an executive are yours. You have the traits of efficiency and capability at your comand, and with them you can carve out a life of prosperity, happiness, and good works. You understand human nature, sympathize with its weaknesses, and are willing to make a career of lending your efforts to the improvement of the lot of mankind.

The cloak of authority is yours, and you seek to use it in an executive capacity in whatever field of endeavor you enter. The larger the group with which you affiliate yourself, the greater will be your accomplishments and rewards. Industry, corporate affairs, and philanthropic organizations can well use your directorial and managerial abilities. Because you lead what Teddy Roosevelt called the strenuous life, you drive yourself hard, and may tend to be dictatorial with others. It is well for you to learn the lesson that efficient management of one's energy is as necessary as the efficient expenditure of one's cash — in other words, get the most out of your investment.

Courage distinguishes you, and your ideal is to see that you and everyone else enjoys freedom of action. You understand the laws of discipline and discrimination, and therefore should "brake" the great destructive force which lies like a sleeping tiger in the inner recess of your personality.

Much of your life is concentrated on the material plane, and therefore your highest expression can be achieved by putting your strongest efforts into dealing with the practical advancement of mankind.

No. 9 Life Cycle
"The Metaphysician"

The highest aspirations and the noblest ideals are your cosmic heritage. Yours is a life of interest in the search for the mysteries behind the veil, and the meaning of psychic and occult experiences. Service is the keynote of your career, for you fully understand that what one does for others, generally and particularly, is the building of the greatest treasure for one's self. All experience is encompassed in the time you have to spend upon this planet, for your Life Cycle is one of the all-inclusive.

You know that love is a greater experience than can be limited to one person or one family or one group. Generosity and perfection are your everlasting goals, and you attempt to reach them through the practice of the divine and occult arts. You understand the great silences, the periods of meditation needed for development, and the need to go into "thy closet and pray."

An extreme sensitivity makes you respond to people, atmosphere, environment, color, voices, and music. Extended to other planes, this trait makes you perceptive and receptive to psychic phenomena. You tend to vacillate between the heights and depths of ecstacy and sadness in your barometer-like reaction to outward circumstances. With the increase in your knowledge of philosophy and occultism, this tendency should vanish into thin air.

Liberty and freedom are your heralds, and you desire to travel upon the path of life unshackled by the impediments of wealth or possessions, knowing that he travels fastest who travels light. In some capacity, you are in touch with the public, or in the public eye, as lecturer, or entertainer, or orator. Your life will be full, and its years should be plenty.

Chapter IV

WHAT DAY WERE YOU BORN?

Each day of the month has its individual numerical vibration. If you were born on the first, second, or any other date up to the thirty-first, your character is molded to a certain degree by the influence of the number of that date.

How does the number of the *day* of your birth differ from that of your Life Cycle? The Life Cycle number is the essential, indestructible individuality. The number of the day of your birth represents you as the world sees you. It is the numerological equivalent of the astrological ascendant or rising sign.

Self-understanding is the key to cosmic power within you. See yourself as others see you, by reading the interpretation of the number of the day of the month you were born.

Remember that the date is for your birthday, irrespective of the month or year you were born. Study this portrait of yourself as others see you so that you may develop your greatest potentialities.

For Those Born on the First Day of Any Month

Courage, initiative, and leadership distinguish you. Where executive ability and organizational powers are needed, you go immediately to the fore. You have an active and brilliant mentality, and a highly creative turn of mind. To follow or obey orders is distasteful to you, and alien to your character. Because you are self-reliant and confident of your abilities, you never hesitate to tackle the most difficult or abstruse of problems. Your undeveloped characteristic is the ability to cooperate with others willingly because the predominating trait in your make-up is your own captaincy. It is well for you to learn to work well with others that you may benefit from the experience as well as improve the impression that you make.

For Those Born On The Second Day of Any Month

You are an excellent helpmate, a perfect partner, and the personification of all that is sought in a collaborator. Your role in the play of life is that of the executor of the plans and projects instituted or originated by others. This does not mean that you lack originality, but that your originality lies in the direction of making ways and means to carry out the blue-print or design made by someone else. You are affectionate by nature, and never hesitate to show your feelings. In every way, you are considerate, unselfish, and always thoughtful of the feelings and wishes of others. Although you are not in the least wishy-washy, you may give that impression because you are so helpful. Your lesson is to avoid letting others take advantage of your good nature.

For Those Born on the Third Day of Any Month

Popularity and contact with large numbers of people occupy your time to a very great extent, for your birthday is significant of dealings with the masses and being in the public eye in some capacity. Cleverness and natural charm bring a lot of friends to you, and you are the center of every group's attention. You make every effort to be charming, for you enjoy the company of other people. You are very versatile — to the extent of sometimes being puzzled as to what form of expression your talents should take. You are, for this reason, somewhat inclined to scatter your talents, and should learn that specialization in a single field of your choice will bring greater rewards than dabbling in many.

For Those Born on the Fourth Day of Any Month

You have a well earned reputation for being thoroughly reliable and trustworthy. In symbolical language, you are like Peter, the rock upon which the Master builded. You are the cosmic mason, the builder who erects the cornerstone and lays the foundations. Your life is an active and creative one, for you are always busy with work that will advance the world, and promote good will among men. You are very practical in your outlook, and succeed brilliantly where success depends upon the handling of material things and affairs. Because you never dodge work, you finish what must be done — and right on schedule. Limited to a certain extent by the activity in your program of life, you must bear in mind the symbol of the number 4, which is the square. It stands for all that is righteous and just in life. It may bound you materially, but within the square of equity you can always rise to great heights.

For Those Born On the Fifth Day of Any Month.

You are mercurial by nature, loving change and variety, and possessing a versatility surpassed by none. The use of words is your natural talent, and you surpass all others in fields where oratory, vocabulary, and the human voice are requisite. Everything you do is characterized by speed, efficiency, and determination. You are volatile as anything in nature, and race through experience after experience, gathering the beauty and the kernel of each to add to the wisdom with which you have been endowed. Nothing can keep you rooted to a single spot, for you must travel far and wide to be happy, and you must travel fast. Keen wit characterizes you, and sometimes you are cutting in your use of it. You can become very distinguished through your talents by applying the brakes when you come to the rough spots on the road of life.

For Those Born On the Sixth Day of Any Month

Your entire existence is a series of progressive steps, for every experience you have is an embodiment of the law of education. You learn at every step, and each one advances you in wisdom, character, and depth of personality. You are deeply attached to your family and home, and one of your fondest dreams is to make every one of your loved ones happy. You willingly accept the responsibilities that are placed upon you, and there are indeed many of them for, recognizing your sterling qualities and willingness, others are not loathe to place the burdens of domesticity upon you. Order and harmony are the passwords of your philosophy of life. To establish these two and then to balance them is your aspiration. It is your belief that love can conquer all, and faith in that ruling passion will surely reward you.

For Those Born on the Seventh Day of Any Month

You have a quiet and unobtrusive nature. More interested in the subtle rather than the brash phases and phenomena of life, you give the impression of being serious and studious. Not many people really know the essential you, for you do not wear you heart on your sleeve, or make a vulgar display of your feelings. You are more interested in mystical and philosophical concepts than in material events or practical matters. You have a deep interest in all that is artistic, and form and composition have a meaning for you that few others gather as quickly as you do. You appreciate the various languges that beauty speaks, and might well be a critic of the plastic, dynamic, and vocal arts. You may be inclined to be somewhat too introspective for a world of crass materiality, but the Creator knows that the world must have its creative dreamers, too.

For Those Born on the Eighth Day of Any Month

You are the personification of the executive branch of the government of life. The organization of the many departments of life needs power, force, and strength — and these you possess to a strongly marked degree. You have the ability to handle all material affairs with great ease, and you specialize in the careful, honest, and efficient manipulation of money matters. When others need help, they turn to you, for you have a deep understanding of the problems of other people, and a deep insight into the cause of their troubles. You are never selfish with your advice or your help. As the head of any large organization, you can lead it toward the accomplishment of its aims, whether they be philanthropic, commercial, or social.

For Those Born on the Ninth Day of Any Month

You are the personification of sympathy and wide understanding. Your vistas are grand, for life to you is as a dome of many colored glass, encompassing all kinds and forms of experience. The harsh, the cruel, the ecstatic, and the rapturous — all float within your ken. You have an unusual psychic sense, and are inclined to have occult experiences that fill you with new knowledge until, at the end of the road of experience, you have at your command the wisdom of the ages. You are a very quick study in the sense that music, art, and literature are all grist to your mill; you grasp their meaning and see their beauty with hardly a conscious effort. Travel will broaden your outlook, and should play an important role in your life. You will cover vast distances, by whatever mode you travel, and the road will eventually lead to tolerance, sympathy, and a universal love.

For Those Born on the Tenth day of any Month

In olden times you might have been an alchemist, because your greatest power is to transmute from one form to another. All forms of change, conversion, and transmutation are your fields of activity. You supply the mental power, agility, and energy to take the river and make it a dynamo. You are the executive in your personality, and can lead to victory where others fear to tread. Creative originality is yours, and you enjoy tackling a good hard problem. You have a strong protective instinct, and though you are positive about everything, you do not mean to do any harm.

You should take care not to become overbearing, for the prestige you now command might suffer if you did.

For Those Born on the Eleventh Day of Any Month

You have an unusually magnetic personality, since the number 11 is considered a master-power number.

Your intuition is highly developed, and you are inspired by high ideals. Electric power almost vibrates from your personal magnetism, and you are generally the master of every situation. Executive ability is prominent in your make-up, and your mind is creative, original, and alert. You seek to shield those you love, and you like the role of the provider.

You value prestige above all things, but because you are sensitive at heart, you are easily wounded. You must learn that the arrows of fortune must sometimes pierce the armor, and everyone has to take as well as give.

For Those Born on the Twelfth Day of Any Month

You have a charming effect on people and a Midas touch on situations. You are a well-balanced person, highly endowed in attractive physical and mental traits. In all things you exercise good judgment, and your actions are motivated by the highest moral and ethical standards. Social life holds a great attraction for you, and you set the pace and create the fads. You have a large capacity for loving, and you are demonstrative with those you love.

You should take the precaution of saving your charms and talents for those occasions when you need them. Your powers are liable to be drained by weaklings if you allow them to be.

For Those Born on the Thirteenth Day of Any Month

You have an infinite capacity for work, which amounts to the classical definition of genius. Leadership of the crowd is yours, and you enjoy your role. It is to your satisfaction that others enjoy your captaincy. The key-note of your thinking and actions is structure. You like to formulate and plan very carefully and then just as carefully carry out. Precision and efficiency mark your efforts, and success crowns them.

You are liable to do too much concentrating. Although you grow in intellectual stature, you must leave energy to bring to flower the spiritual and emotional seeds within you.

For Those Born on the Fourteenth Day of Any Month

You are inspired to spread the truth abroad. Lies, even "white lies," are abhorrent to your nature. The urge within you is to broadcast to the world your beliefs, ideas, and opinions. For this reason you would make an excellent critic. Your good taste and high level of standards can raise the grade of appreciation of all who know and heed you. A vivid and creative mind characterizes you. Your imagination is fertile, and you love change and variety.

In fact, the "spice of life" may be your only indulgence. A love of change, travel, and speed may deter you from accomplishment or specialization; better stay "on the path."

For Those Born on the Fifteenth Day of Any Month

Your home, family, and friends form a circle of affectionate ties which bind you, but in no sense distress you. You have the ability to bear the burden, and the willingness to do it. Matters of education, law, and domesticity are your particular interests. You can be a leader in public speaking, lecturing, and in writing and radio work. Your original ideas in these fields of endeavor can bring you success. Beauty in its various forms appeals to you, and in your way you are a connoisseur.

Too deep a sense of obligation can woo you from looking out for your own welfare. You so willingly help others that your unselfishness can minimize your potentialities. Be kind, but not over-indulgent.

For Those Born on the Sixteenth Day of Any Month

You are clever, alert, and intellectual. Because of the power you have to penetrate the walls of ignorance or abstruse problems, you are inclined to be impatient with dullness. To dominate the scene is no unique experience for you, but you are modest and do not revel in showing off your strength. The subtler things in life appeal to you. On the light side you choose detective stories; on the heavy side you find an interest in all things mystic. You have a great magnetism for people, but you are not too quick to part with your affections.

You should learn to relax with the lighter pleasures of the mind and spirit. Too much concentration inclines you to depression which you must avoid.

For Those Born on the Seventeenth Day of Any Month

You have ambition, courage and vitality. When you extend your best efforts, there is almost nothing of which you are not capable. Success comes to you through your own ideas and a clever way of presenting them to the market-place of the world. You are fortunate in being able to repose and find satisfaction in "inner understanding" and being able to get along with the rest of the world, too. Your mentality and energy put you in the foreground of any field you choose to enter.

Your own timidity may sometimes shock you. This is because you are used to leadership, and sometimes lose sight of the fact that deep within, you are a sensitive human being. However, never lose sight of this core — the best that is in you.

For Those Born on the Eighteenth Day of Any Month

You can run the gamut of emotions and of intellectual qualities. You combine the spiritual, creative, and material in your nature, and might be said to be "all things to all men." Your understanding is inclusive, and no side of life holds either a shock or a surprise for you. In fiduciary matters you display a keen analytical ability. As the treasurer of the funds of others you make an ideal trustee. You demonstrate power in the affairs of men and direct the tides of destiny.

Your depth of comprehension may tend to make you lax in the ways of the world. Since your own ideals are so high, you should take steps never to lose sight of them in order to remain your best self.

For Those Born on the Nineteenth Day of Any Month

Your symbol is the ever turning wheel from creation to completion, and therefore you have experiences of every kind which widen your perceptions and enhance your wisdom. The everlasting emotions of the human race course through your temperament — love, hate, self-preservation. You are very expressive and positive in word, act, and feeling. Fortune follows you, but as adventure beckons, you are likely to pick up and travel on to other pasures.

This is your lesson: to learn to let the benefits accrue so that the uncertainties of life will never leave you high or dry.

For Those Born on the Twentieth Day of Any Month

What you do is done with a will, for you have reached a stage of inner development that it is the privilege of few to attain. You are sought out by others to give of yourself — in every sense — out of soul, spirit, mentality and purse. You answer each call for help willingly, for such is your nature. When the Creator of Universal Law wants his edicts fulfilled, you are the executive branch of the domain. You are warm-hearted, affectionate, and loyal. No contingency finds you unprepared.

You must beware not to devote all your efforts to the welfare of others. In the course of events, you may require the energy and talents you have disbursed on others; conserve them for your own good.

For Those Born on the Twenty-first Day of Any Month

You are considered lucky because you have good fortune, an interesting personality, and a magnetic way about you. While you think for yourself, you are not unmindful of the help others need, and you cooperate. The lighter and glittering side of life appeals to you, and you are the center of the social circle. You like many people, and you are popular with both sexes. Your talents are numerous, and you know how to fit into every sphere in business, home, and socially.

Don't fritter away the gifts with which you have been endowed. Learn how to spread your charm and talents a little thin, so there will be vitality left to accomplish your own purposes.

For Those Born on the Twenty-second Day of Any Month

Power, vibrancy, and force characterize you, for

you are ruled by the master-power number 22. You might be called "the Master- builder." Plans, projects, the vistas of human endeavor, are all within your ken and within your capability to achieve. Doubts rarely assail you, for you have the self-confidence innate in those highly endowed intellectually and emotionally. You can be of great help when called upon, and it does not take too much away from your own interests.

You may be inclined to be over-conservative in carrying out inspirational programs. Do not become cloistered in the conduct of your life. You have so much to give and gain — go and build!

For Those Born on the Twenty-third Day of Any Month

You are highly emotional and changeable. Your temperament is truly mercurial, and this gives you an interesting personality, even if it is somewhat unpredictable. Your vocabulary is extensive, and you express yourself well in many ways — speaking, writing, singing, lecturing, teaching, demonstrating, and acting. Small spaces make you feel confined. You love your freedom and let nothing bind you. You are quick to express your devotion, and you gather many admirers.

Your love of fast-moving vehicles and fast methods of doing things should be carefully watched. Don't give up the solid virtues and ways for fleeting attractions which may have a magnetic call for you.

For Those Born on the Twenty-fourth Day of Any Month

Your greatest happiness is in spreading happiness to others. You feel that no greater delight can come to anyone than through learning, and you are the teacher.

Combined in your make-up are the cooperator and the builder. This makes life a serious business for you, but you get joy in creative activity and do not resent the restrictions of a busy life. Home and family mean more to you than anything else. No glittering entertainment attracts you as much as the easy chair and fireside. You want to be surrounded by the finer, beautiful things of life, and you make an effort to get them.

Don't assume every obligation that is passed on to you. Your willingness would soon make you an easy mark for those not eager to hold up their end.

For Those Born on the Twenty-fifth Day of Any Month

You are the seeker of truth. You life is a search for the grail of sincerity, loyalty, honesty, and all the finer things. In character you are intellectually superior and emotionally well-developed. In fact, the subtler emotions and the mysteries of the subconscious are perfectly clear to you, so penetrating is your understanding. You are imaginative, quiet, and somewhat of a sphinx to your family and acquaintances. Action with you takes a slow but final course, and your path may have more delays and disappointments than you like. However, you have patience, and you eventually achieve your goal.

Don't ever lose or sacrifice your high ideals. Your comprehension of the mystic principles that make men tick will bolster up your spirit when material affairs seem intolerable.

For Those Born on the Twenty-sixth Day of Any Month

You are endowed with a vital and energetic nature;

power emanates from you as it does from a dynamo. Combined with this force are cooperation and an urge to teach others all you know. You are especially concerned with the welfare of your home and loved ones. Big deals have a fascination for you, and you are happy when engaged in any form of corporate employment or direction. Your executive ability can be put to good use as a club counselor or in your own business. Although you are affectionate, you are not particularly demonstrative.

It might be said of you that "You don't know your own strength." This might lead you to be overbearing with your sense of power; curb this tendency.

For those Born on the Twenty-seventh Day of Any Month

The course of your life includes a very wide variety of experience. You are intellectual, perceptive, sympathetic, and a deep thinker. Strong powers of imagination and visualization are yours. Long-range projects fascinate you, and all matters of distance and dimension intrigue you. A career dealing with travel, railroads, ships, telegraphy, or television should prove successful for you. Occult mysteries appeal to you, and you could develop into a profound scholar along these lines.

Avoid leading too cloistered a life. Self-interest might lead to introspection amounting almost to manic egotism, so avoid it.

For Those Born in the Twenty-eighth Day of Any Month

You have the initiative and leadership to be one of the foremost of all number groups. Cosmic forces are strong in your makeup, and you express them in work of an organizational nature. You are creative and original in your ideas, but you can do better with a collaborator or partner than you do alone. The power to make beneficial changes is yours, and you might do well in the material practice of chemistry, physics, and other natural sciences. The same ability extends to transforming ideas into practical projects, and can even be extended to your emotional life.

Do not be too independent in your thoughts or actions. If you are considered completely self-sufficient, you may lose the warmth of the friendships you now possess.

For Those Born on the Twenty-ninth Day of Any Month

A powerful magnet is the core of your personality, and you gather unto yourself a flock of friends. You have the faculty of being such a social success that you may be spoiled by attention. You are cooperative but in an intellectual rather than a warm-hearted way. Experience adds to the instinct you have innately within you for understanding others. Your wide perception makes you a citizen of the universe. In your home life you have a deep interest, and you see that provision for all necessaries is made.

You may be inclined to reflect the personalities of your acquaintances. Do not be too accommodating or too willful. Moderation is the keynote of your best expression.

For Those Born on the Thirtieth Day of Any Month

Social life is the meat and drink of your life. This does not imply that there is no serious side to your nature, for you have a conscientious soul that seeks to fullfill every duty of your career. The power of attraction is strongly emphasized in your number chart, and you will never lack friends and counselors. Seek to put your magnetism to the fullest use by giving your services to large clubs or organizations or contributing them to service clubs.

Your potentialities are great; do not fritter away your talents, charms, or money where they will go to waste, instead of in quarters where they will be appreciated.

For Those Born on the Thirty-first
Day of Any Month

You have creative ideas and the connections to have them carried out by the right people. Although you restrict yourself somewhat by sticking to routine and schedule, you can be a glorius social leader. Judgment and discrimination dictate the conduct you know to be best for you. You can always depend on your good taste to put you in the right mood in the right atmosphere. Your type of conscientiousness never goes unrewarded.

Look out for your own interests more than you do. Your unselfish actions and attitude may lead you to play the game too much without thoughts of playing to win for yourself.

Chapter V

THE HOURLY CYCLES

The Hourly Cycle takes its vibratory power from the number of the hour approaching. Thus, from 6 to 7 o'clock, the hourly cycle is number 7. From 7 to 8 o'clock, you have an 8 Hourly Cycle. All numbers are reduced to a single digit. The number of each Hourly Cycle is given in the table below:

TIME		CYCLE NUMBER
12 to 1 o'clock	....	1
1 to 2 "	....	2
2 to 3 "	....	3
3 to 4 "	....	4
4 to 5 "	....	5
5 to 6 "	....	6
6 to 7 "	....	7
7 to 8 "	....	8
8 to 9 "	....	9
9 to 10 "	....	1
10 to 11 "	....	2
11 to 12 "	....	3

Naturally, these influences are universal. Thus, from 8 to 9 o'clock a.m., a 9-Cycle, most people are ending the activities of early morning and preparing for a long day ahead. That is the influence of number 9 — to put an end to one thing and prepare for the next. From 12 to 1 p.m. is a number 1 Hourly Cycle. This is the usual time for lunch. The number 1 is new; it is active. It is starting out the new activities of the afternoon program. Often, at lunch, new plans are discussed and new projects begun.

You can ascertain whether an Hourly Cycle is favorable for specific plans, work, or activity. If the number of your Individual Day is the same as the number of the Hourly Cycle, it is favorable for certain types of activity. In the next chapter, you will learn how to find out what vibrancy you have in your Individual Day. Then, in the explanations given, you can find the individual activities favored in each Hourly Cycle. The matters favored by the Hourly Cycles are the same as those favored by the Individual Days. Consult the list of topics and the explanations in the next chapter.

Chapter VI

THE DAILY CYCLES

You respond to the vibrations of numbers at all times. For guidance in the use of the daily numerical influences, you should know the number of your Individual Day. The directions for finding the number of your Individual Day are given herewith.

To Find Your Individual Day

To find your Daily Cycle or, more accurately, your Individual Day, you do some simple arithmetic. Find the sum of the numbers of the following dates, and reduce them to a single digit:

The number of your month of birth =
    (January = 1; February = 2; etc.)
The number of your day of birth =
The present calendar year =
The number of the current calendar month =
The number of the current calendar day =

                —————
           Total =

Add each number of this total together and reduce to a single digit. For example: If you were born on February 22 (any year), and today is March 15, 1944:

The number of your month of birth February, is 2   2
The number of your day of birth 22
The present calendar year 1944
The number of the current calendar month, March   3
The number of tre current calendar day 15
               Total = 1986

The total 1986 equals 1 plus 9 plus 8 plus 6 equals 24; 2 +4 = 6. Thus, 6 is the number of your Individual Day.

Calendar Days

You now have the key to getting the number vibrancy of your Individual Day. You must not overlook the Universal Day number vibrancy derived from adding the numbers of the day together, and then reducing them to a single digit. For example: if today is March 15, 1944.

                    March (third month)   3
                    Day of month   15
                    Year 1944
                                    Total =1962

1962 equals 1 plus 9 plus 6 plus 2 equals 18; 1 + 8 = 9. This makes it a 9 Calendar Day.

The number of the Calendar Day influences everyone, everywhere. For this reason, it is well to consider what your Individual Day is, compared to the Calendar Day. If your Individual Day vibrancy is the same as the Calendar Day vibrancy, it is favorable for your plans and actions.

Every day is favorable to certain kinds of activity, not auspicious for others. Your Individual Days have their good and adverse aspects.

Get the most out of each day by applying knowledge and intelligence to universal forces.

1. Compute the number of the Calendar Day.
2. Compute the number of your Individual Day.
3. Look up the significance of your Individual Day.
4. Ask yourself: Is this a favorable cycle?
    If it really is, your answer will be yes, and the next step will be:
5. Do it!

The activities favored on the Calendar Days are the same as those favored on Individual Days, but apply universally. Consult the lists and explanations given below.

> CAUTION — Do your arithmetic accurately, or your results will be to no avail.

SIGNIFICANCE OF THE DAILY CYCLES

These Interpretations apply especially to your Individual Days, and also to the Hourly Cycles and Calendar Days.

Number 1 Vibrancy

On a 1-Individual Day, you should awake with new energy, fine spirits, and an eagerness to leap out of bed and get things started. 1 is the number of beginning, of creative ideas, and productive activities. It indicates that a 9 day cycle has come to an end, so you should put the concerns of those 9 days behind you. Let your attitude be one of welcoming new ideas, new activities, new experiences, and new acquaintances.

You are liable to be inspired with splendid ideas about business and management of the home. If you have been cross with someone, you are now inclined to consider the argument trivial and forget it. You make new acquaintances, whom you welcome to your circle, and who become lasting friends. This is a favorable cycle to seek advancement in social and business ventures. You may run for office, or seek a raise in salary, with success.

The 1-Vibrancy Cycle presents favorable aspects for:

Selling business ideas.
Getting a raise in salary.
Interviews with father, brother, or employer.
Making things with your hands.
Furthering your ambitions.
Seeking a new job.
Starting a new book.
Musical composition.
Registering for a course of study.
Making new friends.
Embarking on a journey.
Entering a contest.
Planting — in proper season.
Trying out for a part in a play.
All artistic and creative work.
Installing new machinery.
Taking walks or hikes.
Seeking office in clubs.
Selling subscriptions.

Number 2 Vibrancy

Cooperation is the clue to the temperament, character, and personality of the 2-Cycle. It is a good time to ask for favors. Equally, you will be inclined to grant any favor asked of you, and this will ingratiate you with the person you show such kindness. Affairs will progress slowly, and hustle and bustle will not be in evidence. Thus, the very pace of things gives the time, and the temper gives the ability, to develop tact. Diplomacy is the order of the day — no arguments, back-talk, or aggression.

You probably get along better with women than with men in a 2-Cycle. It is well to keep control of things in your own hands, however, for you might give the impression of being timid or deceitful. Someone may confide a matter of great secrecy in you. Be sure not to divulge the confidences you receive, as it would only have a bad effect on you. Use left-overs and materials on hand today. Don't go shopping for a lot of new things. Whatever your intuition tells you may well be depended upon.

The 2-Vibrancy Cycle presents favorable aspects for:

Requesting and granting favors.

Interviews with mother, sister, female relatives.

Marriage proposals.

Raising funds.

Getting a man to build a home.

Exercising and enhancing charm.

Making tactful speeches.

Getting popularity by being a good listener.

Employing discrimination.

Number 3 Vibrancy

In a 3-Cycle you will find yourself giving full expression to all that is in you. There will be no repressions or inhibitions, only the will to success and happiness. Other people seek you out, and you want to become a part of a group.

This is a fine aspect for work with organizations and corporations. It is equally good for clubs, societies, and parties; and you can play a leading part in their activities. If you are in public life, or your job puts you in touch with large numbers of people, this is a very favorable time for you. Should your desires be in the direction of such work, this is an auspicious time to forward your ambitions.

Love and affection rule during a 3-Cycle, and you will be swayed by sentiment toward your loved ones as well as by emotions of a romantic nature. You will be thrilled by the pleasures derived from appreciation of the arts. However, the 3-Cycle has the effect of making you want to play. It provides time for enjoyment, but your desire for it may know no bounds and urge you on to squander time, talent, and money. Do nothing that you can not really afford to do.

The 3-Vibrancy Cycle presents favorable aspects for:

> Beginning a bank account.
> Buying government securities.
> Asking for a special favor.
> Checking your possessions.
> Presenting a letter of recommendation.
> Beginning a new study course.
> Buying seasonal gifts.
> Attending to a legal matter.
> Submitting writing to editors.

Number 4 Vibrancy

The 4-Individual Day is one of building. In this cycle, you are symbolized as enclosed within a square; consequently, the only way you can grow is "up." Therefore, all your acts will be such as are planned for future effect. You may feel confined or restricted. That is because you are giving up immediate pleasures for future benefits.

All work of an organizing nature and all work concerned with large organizations should find success in a 4-Cycle. The 4-Day is cold and intellectual in temperament, and your activity, while productive, is slow.

Plans for saving, for founding a home, and for children are uppermost in the mind. This is well, because you can take advantage of the strength, stability, and power which are symbolized by the building 4.

The 4-Vibrancy Cycle presents favorable aspects for:

Laying the cornerstone of any important project.
Arranging school affairs of children.
Providing yourself with long-wearing clothes.
Fixing up your home.
Signing long-term contracts.
Checking up on your health.
Renting a safety-deposit vault.
Entering a partnership.
Dealing in earth or mining commodities.

Number 5 Vibrancy

The 5-Cycle denotes change. It may well be that whatever you have planned for this day will go awry. A really fine way to meet the 5-Day is with no plans at all; then whatever happens is not upsetting.

There is a great deal of motion in the 5. Activity and speed appeal to you on these days. May, the fifth month, is the time for much changing of residence, for example. October, the tenth month, two 5's, is even more active in the moving business. The 5-Days are similar. You may find yourself changing things around, moving furniture, hurrying here and there.

Talk, conversation, and argument are also part of the 5-Cycle. Sir James M. Barrie calls conversation "what men live by." The negative of this is argument — what men die by. They are both in the 5. However, it is a fine cycle for entertainment. You can enjoy theatre and movie parties. The cycle is also good for lectures, concerts, writing, and radio.

The 5-Vibrancy Cycle presents favorable aspects for:

> Writing letters and all forms of communication.
> Enjoying a hike or a short trip.
> Trying out for a part in a play.
> Reasoning with children.
> Making new acquaintances.
> Listening to radio entertainment.
> Taking beauty treatment.
> Making a public debut.
> Planning a study course.
> Planning a neighborhood party.

Number 6 Vibrancy

The 6-Cycle is one of reasonable happiness. The day should provide all you need though nothing to waste. You will feel joyous, and the spirit of lightening' the burden of others will be in you. Sharing the labor of those you love and accepting responsibilities for their care may be your delight.

Harmony, rhythm, beauty, and culture are part of the make-up of the 6-Cycle. In the home, in married life, and in relations with neighbors there is a charm.

All matters dealing with the home and with education are in the province of the 6. You may plan schooling for children, and for yourself. Consider how best you may learn — whether it be in a regular school or the school of experience. The 6-Cycle tells you, "All is well."

The 6-Vibrancy Cycle presents favorable aspects for:

Beauty culture and developing grace and charm.

Home study and correspondence courses.

Flower culture.

Falling in love.

Dealing with groups of people.

Proposing marriage.

Speaking on the radio.

Making up old quarrels.

Studying any form of art.

Consulting fashion experts.

Number 7 Vibrancy

On your 7-Individual Day, you will probably want to be alone. The 7-Cycle is quiet, peaceful, calm, and mysterious in its nature. You will probably take some time to meditate and resolve on inner or spiritual concerns.

Your external acts and conduct will most likely be along inventive lines. Your ideas for devices, gadgets, systems, and efficiency should be excellent and may prove profitable.

The responsibilities of your home will be a matter for your consideration. You may have something of importance to go over with your family, probably with your parents.

If you are interested in philosophy or art, you will find the 7-Cycle a splendid time to study and to express yourself along these lines.

The 7-Vibrancy Cycle presents favorable aspects for:

Making specific decisions about your personal life.

Consulting people in positions of authority.

Considering the purchase of property.

Adopting a child.
Beginning psychic studies.
Making wedding plans.
Rest, meditation, and prayer.
Taking care of domestic matters.
Checking on your diet.
Avoiding scandal and gossip.

Number 8 Vibrancy

The 8-Individual Cycle is one in which you can express all the material desires. The 8-Vibrancy is the number of wealth and power. You can take the lead on your 8-Day, and others will follow you. Energy and will are in your cycle, and you can take advantage of feeling strong and more courageous.

All money matters come under the rule of 8. You should attend to matters concerning savings, investments, stocks, securities, bonds, mortgages, and insurance.

Don't forget to use some of the pep you have on an 8-Day to help someone else. Bear in mind that one of the best ways to benefit yourself is by following the rule of 8: Help others to help themselves.

The 8-Vibrancy Cycle presents favorable aspects for:

Settling monetary matters.
Relying on your intuition.
Seeking advice from a spiritual mentor.
Exercising authority with tact.
Dealing with charitable institutions.
Seeking election to any office.
Attending to matters of employment.
Visiting with loved ones.

Making yourself attractive.

Demonstrating your diplomacy.

Number 9 Vibrancy

The 9-Individual Day has the very best aspects, and therefore, in its negative expression, the very worst aspects. You may be, on your 9-Day, like the little girl with the little curl in the nursery rhyme; very, very good, or very, very bad.

The temperament of the 9-Cycle is sincere, truthful, noble, vivid, creative, vital, and well-balanced. You will not compromise on your 9-Day.

You may plan long journeys, send telegrams, write letters, or perform any service connected with long distance successfully.

The 9-Cycle is also the most auspicious for the study of occult subjects.

The 9-Vibrancy Cycle presents favorable aspects for:

Long journeys.

Getting help in correcting errors of your own.

All secret and confidential matters.

Doing charitable work.

Getting publicity for worthy causes.

Victory in a competition.

Creative art work.

Music appreciation.

Studying the occult.

Chapter VII

YOUR INDIVIDUAL MONTH

As the year progresses from month to month, you advance with it. Each month of progress encompasses a cycle of influence. The broader trends of life are encompassed in your Individual Yearly Cycle (explained in the next chapter); the narrower influences are encompassed in the Daily Cycles. For immediate needs and aims, the Daily Cycle influences should be heeded. For the more distant goals, the annual or Yearly Cycles should be heeded, while for the intermediate, or proximate goals, the influence of the number of your Individual Month should be followed.

How To Find Your Individual Month Number

To compute the number vibration of your Individual Month Cycle, add together the number of the current calendar month, the number of your Individual Year Cycle, and the number of months back to your last birthday. Then reduce this total to a single digit.

Outline for the above steps:

Number	Number of current calendar month.———
of your	Day of your birth . . . .———
Individual	Month of your birth . . . .———
Year	Number of months back to birthday ———
	Total. . . . . .———

Example:

Let us assume that this is the month of December, 1945; and that you were born January 19, 1909. The above outline would be filled in as follows:

Number of current calendar month (December)   3
Day of your birth   19
Month of your birth (January)   1
Year of your birth 1909
Number of months back to last birthday   11
Total.... 1943

Reduce the total to a single digit as follows:
1 plus 9 plus 4 plus 3 equal 17; 1 plus 7 equal 8.

Thus, the month of December, 1945 would be an 8 Individual Month Cycle.

Compute your Individual Month Cycle, and find the guidance and interpretation for the vibration of it in the explanatory paragraphs below.

No. 1 Individual Month Cycle

An excellent number, denoting the opening of a new cycle. Initiative and independence are to the fore. Influences which prevented your having your own way previously are no longer obstacles in your path. Leadership and forcefulness bring compensatory rewards: success and achievement. New business enterprises, new associations, and new ideas should prosper. Concentrate on buying and selling, advertising, merchandising, publicity, and creative work for profit. New friendships should be formed, and prove a source of much pleasure to you. Social success should bring you happiness and popularity. The new strength arising within you revitalizes your personality, as No. 1 is the significator of all things new.

No. 2 Individual Month Cycle

Now is the time to cooperate with others to the full of your capacity, rather than to start any new project. You should learn many valuable lessons, both in formal education and in the school of experience. A friendship may blossom into romance, or may turn into a prosperous collaboration. Yours will be the role of the matchmaker and the one to reconcile those who have quarreled. Keep your temper at an even level; don't fly off the handle for any reason. Minor changes may take place in your routine, but these will come as the result of the suggestions of others. You may feel during this month that you are vacillating, or that you are unable to make up your mind about a vital issue. Should that be the case, defer any important decision until the next Month Cycle.

No. 3 Individual Month Cycle

Success should attend your efforts this month. Social popularity should bring you a lot of pleasure and, in fact, you may fritter away more time than practiticable on parties. Be careful not to squander your money, as the temptation to play may be very strong. As the inspired leader of a group, you may find yourself in advanced prestige. During this cycle, you should find increased pleasure and appreciation in the arts, particularly in literature. You should also try to express yourself well in words and oratorically, for the power to do so will be increased at this time. Optimism fills the environment which you occupy, and you should enjoy it and prosper in it.

No. 4 Individual Month Cycle

This is a month of work and achievement. You may be circumscribed in your actions and limited in your pleasures, but at the end of the month you will be able to look back upon a real cycle of accomplishment. Your mental outlook should be that of the person saving up present money and pleasures for the greater enjoyment of the future; in other words, this is a time of storing and building up. You may now lay the foundations for effective achievement of plans you have let lie fallow in your mind. Bring out the ideas that you have been fostering and express them now, or prepare a campaign that will bring them to fruition in the future.

No. 5 Individual Month Cycle

This month is a period of change and adjustment, althongh both the change and adjustment may be of brief duration. Even though temporary in nature, you should be prepared to see a lot of action that may require your rendering your mental attitude one of readiness. The home situation may go through minor changes, or there may be a change in the personnel therein. Your employment situation may improve provided you are ready to be advanced. This can be accomplished by the wise use of your mentality, particularly the wise choice of words in dealing with your employer, supervisor, or even your assistants and co-workers. Do not neglect this opportunity to express yourself brilliantly and fully. Let the orator in you come out. Advertise your wares, and seek favorable publicity. Meet this cycle of change with open arms.

No. 6 Individual Month Cycle

This cycle is the embodiment of the laws of material supply and education. For this reason, this month is one in which you will not have to worry particularly about the source of your income. However, you may have to share it, for the law of education implies the necessity of learning the lesson of unselfish-

ness and accepting your responsibilities. Try to enhance the beauty of your surroundings, for the vibrations are favorable for the increase of enjoyment
through the decorative arts. While you will have to
adopt a realistic and adult attiude toward your tasks
and duties, you will also have the pleasure to be gained
from a feeling of cofidence and a deep sense of appreciation of all that is lovely in nature and in art.

No. 7 Individual Month Cycle

The more serious aspects of life will probably have
a stronger appeal for you this month than will the
frivolous or temporary pleasures. You can now study
yourself, your friends, and your environment with a
detachment that is cool and clear. Be grateful for this
chance to see things as they are, for it gives you the
opportunity to evaluate that does not exist when you
are in an emotional mood. Be prepared to cast off the
impediments of life that are not worth your while.
Make the decision to study, and let your field of study
be broad. Life itself as well as its population and cus-
toms are as valuable fields of investigation as the arts
and crafts, not to say vocational subjects. Mystic studies should also attract you during this month, and you
should have some marked degree of success in the
investigation of the hidden side of nature.

No. 8 Individual Month Cycle

Power and energy are yours during the month
when the 8 vibration reigns. This is a cycle in which
you should assume the direction of all the affairs with
which you are connected. All business deals should follow the pattern that you design, whether you are a
tycoon or just a housewife who does the daily market-

ing. Play the role of the director, for this is your cosmic function under the present influence. Make achievement your aim of the month; now is the time to show the world (as well as yourself) that you have the determination to fulfill every one of your potentialities. Do not forget the plight of those less fortunate than yourself during this time of success and prosperity. It is truly more blessed to give than to receive, and this blessing may be yours among the others of the month.

No. 9 *Individual Month Cycle.*

This is an excellent month if you use its numerical vibration for the correct purpose, and that is to get rid of old habits of thought and action that are deterring your progress. Keep in communication with persons who are far away, as this may lead to an unexpected opportunity. Spend at least a part of the time in the study of occult subjects, for the number 9 rules the study of the mysteries behind the veil. You may have surprising psychic experiences, and your intuition should surely be very keen. Do not seek outside advice, for the answer to your immediate problems lies within yourself. Consider this as a period set aside for casting off the useless, and preparing to begin anew. Face the next cycle with optimism and confidence.

Chapter VIII

YOUR INDIVIDUAL YEAR CYCLE

The ceaselessly changing phenomena of nature are ordered and, because they are ordered, they can be predicted. The cyclic nature of all things makes prophecy possible. The astronomer can tell you the position of the planets a hundred years hence. The meteorologist can tell you the time of the tides, the hours of the sunshine, and the season of the tempest. The physician can tell you the course of a fever and prognosticate its end. The astrologer can interpret the aspects in your horoscope, and the numerologist can foreshadow the trends and tendencies of the numerical cycles through which you will pass, and how you can respond to them.

Your reaction to universal tempo depends upon the date of your birth. You might visualize the number power of cycles as the radio-active waves sent forth into the ether by a powerful broadcasting station. The waves surround you in all of space, but your response to them depends on your receiving set, which is your own number. Your "reception" will be different from that of a person with a different "set" of numbers.

It is a very simple matter to calculate your Individual Year number. Briefly, all you need do is add the number value of your month of birth, date of birth (regardless of the year), and the present calendar year, and then reduce the total to a single digit.

Number Values of Each Month

January	1	July	7
February	2	August	8
March	3	September	9
April	4	October	1
May	5	November	2
June	6	December	3

For example: If you were born on November 13 (in any year) you add:

The number value of your month of birth (Nov.)   2
The day of your birth 13
The present calendar year 1945

Total = 1960

Then reduce the total to a single digit, as follows: 1960 equals 1 plus 9 plus 6 plus 0 equals 16; 16 equals 1 plus 6 equals 7. Thus your year number for 1945 would be 7. You would then read the interpretation for the number 7 in the paragraphs below.

Calculate your Individual Year number according to these simple rules. When you have computed this number, look for it in the paragraphs below, and use the interpretation as a guide throughout the year.

No. 1 Year Interpretation

This cycle finds you ready for new beginnings. You should be able to assert yourself, exercise your initiative and demonstrate your leadership.

Make plans, and put them into action. New business propositions should be given your most serious consideration, for it is likely that you will make a change which will eventually prove profitable to you. Welcome all new associates that you meet in business and socially because these people will become lasting friends.

Your mental outlook will be of major importance throughout the year. Welcome change and all that is novel. Look forward to a new nine-year cycle with enthusiasm and a receptive attitude.

Your creative and inventive powers are at their peak, and you should therefore concentrate on producing results. Study, writing, merchandising, mechanical arts, creative arts, and invention should lead to prestige and profit.

You can be a pioneer this year. Promote your favorite ambition, for cosmic forces are working with you. Travel is likely to take part of your time.

You should have interesting and stimulating experiences. This cycle is also under the planetary rulership of the Sun, so you can shine brilliantly.

No. 2 Year Iinterpretation

Your magnetism will attract new friends and experiences to you. A receptive, cooperative attitude will bring you much more than an aggressive one. Do not be impatient; your cue for fulfillment is waiting and watching.

Partnerships evolve and prosper in the 2-Cycle. By being on the alert for a collaborator, life-mate, or business associate, and forming a union, you can further you ambition. However, you will have to exercise your judgment and discrimination, for deceit is in the air, and you may be taken in.

You may feel weighed down by a burden of details. It is wiser to work out minor aspects than to launch big, new projects at this time. Acquire all the information, knowledge, and skills that you can because this is a fertile period for self-improvement.

Important matters on the emotional plane may be exaggerated. You may find it difficult to maintain an even balance in your relations with older people or parents unless you retain an absolutely calm front. Accept this for what it is—a challenge, as well as a chance, to develop your tact and diplomacy.

This is a splendid cycle for building: you can construct a new home, or a mansion for your soul.

No. 3 *Year Interpretation*

The number 3 is indicative of a cycle of fruition or success. Yet you must not consider this year merely "lucky" because the negative aspect of the number 3 tends to make you scatter your harvest, whether that be money, talents, or associations.

Social success will be yours. Your popularity will grow as your personality becomes expansive under the successful and stimulating rays of the combination of the planet Jupiter and number 3. Your friends will not only rally around you for the good times you have together, but to be of assistance with advice, with money, and with moral backing.

Self-expression is the form your power will take. You should therefore be careful of what you say and write, and examine carefully any agreements or other documents requiring your signature. Put this force to a creative use by being original in your spoken and written words, and seek tangible profits from them. You can market whatever you put into words, whether the product is a story, play, script, or idea.

This is a selling cycle for you. You should profit by

clever merchandising and the furtherance of efficiency plans. Sell the commodities you no longer need or which you neglected because you thought they had no value. Seek a market now.

This is a cycle set aside for your enjoyment and success. Make the most of it.

No. 4 Year Interpretation

To you will accrue the strength and energy to work during your 4-Cycle because the vibratory power of 4 is a building force. The symbol of the number 4 is a square, within which you are standing. Naturally, this restricts you as far as expansion is concerned, but it does not prevent you from growing in the upward direction.

Your material affairs should prosper, and you should be able to build a solid foundation for security in the years to come by the proper connections, accomplishments, and saving. Should you feel overburdened, think of the rewards and compensations that your present sacrifices of good times are storing up for the future.

Romantic and emotional matters may seem submerged at present, but this really is a fine cycle for the establishment of firm friendships, for balancing family relationships, and for becoming engaged or married. The serious side of your relationships with other people will be emphasized, while the light or gay side will prove rather unimportant.

Do not waste any of your forces on complaining, on activities which bring no positive results, or on resisting the impositions of your 4-Cycle. An inward glow of spiritual enlightenment will illuminate the "heavy" cycle. Keep the symbol of the 4-square in mind, remembering that you can grow *up*.

No. 5 Year Interpretation

This cycle is one of change and motion, under the numerical rulership of 5 and the planetary rulership of Mercury. The indications for you are indeed pleasant.

It is likely that you will travel some time during the year, either for business or pleasure. More probably, this will be related to a vacation to which you have looked forward for some time, and which is now materializing.

The stimulating vibratory forces encourage the use of words. You will discover renewed powers of eloquence which can sway your audience, whether it be small or large. Enterprises which are favorable for you are lecturing, teaching, writing, dramatics, radio, and all communications industries, such as advertising, telephone, telegraphy, and postal service.

You will receive added pleasure from intellectual pursuits, as though the gateway to chambers of your mind were suddenly opened to receive new information, knowledge, and understanding. Study, reading, theatricals, music, and exercise will comprise the activity of your hours of ease.

Do not try to restrain your friendly and social impulses. Seek people out. Go places and do things. You now have the opportunity to reap the reward of work done in previous cycles, so enjoy yourself.

No. 6 Year Interpretation

Whether you are at home or away from home during this cycle, your mind will be occupied by domestic matters. It is likely that you will have to assume responsibilities that you may not have had up to now. Be prepared to direct the affairs of the members of your family, to balance the budget, to care for the furnishings, and to provide for the household needs.

This is not as discouraging or burdensome as it may seem at first, for you will be the recipient of cosmic assistance. Thus, you will be enabled to create beauty and establish harmony in your surroundings.

The employment outlook for your cycle is excellent. You should be free of occupational and financial problems because of the beneficent and protective power of number 6. It may be difficult to save any large amounts, but all immediate needs should be well provided for. Have faith in the symbolism of the 6 which stands for the law of supply, which brings money to those who make an effort.

Educational matters progress in this cycle. Teaching is favored. Learning, whether in the school of experience, in an academic or vocational institution, or through a home study course, should further your ambition.

Marital affairs should provide the happiness that comes of harmony and rhythm. Comfort and culture in your surroundings should form a perfect blend of the intellectual and the emotional aspects of your Individual Year Cycle.

No. 7 Year Interpretation

The "peace that passeth all understanding" can be yours during your 7-Cycle if you respond to the numerical vibrancy which influences you. This should be easily accomplished because the number 7 is intellectual by nature, and should stimulate your mental potentialities.

The pace of your affairs will most likely be slow. Delays are in store in business and financial matters, and you should therefore cultivate a philosophical attitude toward them. Your physical energy may be lowered also, and you must avoid overindulgence of any kind to prevent serious consequences.

Neglect nothing that deals with distance, for unexpected good fortune may lie in that direction. Keep up your correspondence with friends and relatives who are far away. If you are starting on a career, it would be well to choose one dealing with travel or communications.

The transitory pleasures of social life will not have too great an appeal for you because you will be more attracted by the universal verities. Philosophy and mysticism come to the forefront under the number 7 influence. Meditation and the study of mysticism have a strong attraction for you now, and they bring you keen intuitive powers and spiritual enlightenment.

No. 8 Year Interpretation

Energy and force are bestowed upon you during your 8-Cycle. You should use this power in a creative and constructive way, exercising your discrimination that you may do so, for the dynamic vibrancy of the number 8 can be destructive in its negative aspects.

"Big business" is ruled by 8, and the implications to you are success in your financial and business affairs. However, the law of compensation requires you to think of others as well as of yourself. Philanthropy is under the governorship of the number 8; since you are probably not professionally engaged in charitable work, you should volunteer at least part of your time and services to a worthwhile philanthropic organization.

Take your place in the world of affairs, and do it with confidence in yourself. All your executive powers are to the fore this year, and you should be able to command any situation.

Greater freedom will be yours this year than you have ever had for quite a long time. Endurance and power issue from the dynamo that is your personality. Do not let this force operate undiciplined by your judgment and experience.

Your greatest reward may come to you in the form of the satisfaction you get from knowing that your conduct is ethical and that you are making an effort to improve not yourself alone, but mankind.

No. 9 Year Interpretation

Since your cycle number is the highest vibration of the single digits, you may expect a variety of experiences. The number 9 represents the closing of a nine year cycle, and this indicates the end of one type of living and the beginning of another with renewed hope and enthusiasm. Your psychological attitude towards this year's vibrations is very important. You should cultivate the attitude that all things come to an end — but to make way for the new.

One important feature of the year is that your psychic powers and intuitive receptivity will be thrown open. You should discover soon after the start of the year that you can rely confidently upon your impressions. Along the same lines, you will find an increasing interest in things occult. The number 9 is the ruler of occultism, and this is a propitious cycle in which to further your studies along these lines, to investigate psychic phenomena, and to strengthen your ties with the infinite.

Take advantage of this closing to cast off old modes of thought, wasteful ways, and non-constructive habits.

Take advantage, on the positive side, to acquire all the culture, knowledge, and appreciation of the arts that the number 9 favors.

Now that you are coming to the end of a lengthy cycle in your life, you may look to the rewards of the years of activity they comprised. Happiness, love, and, perhaps greatest of all, understanding, should crown your life in this cycle.

Chapter IX

THE FOUR-MONTH CYCLES

The daily ebb and flow of the tide, the day following the night, the phases of the moon, all are wonderful examples of the potent laws of nature which govern life in cycles.

Every cycle is numbered. From its number, its significance can be interpreted. Each great historical era down to each hour in a person's life is a cycle, designated by a number, and therefore to be understood. Indeed, all things are to be understood from their numerical portent. "The very hairs of your head are all numbered," says Matthew, x:30.

The four-month cycles in your life are numbered according to a plan based on the date of your birth. Your individual year, in other words, is counted from one birthday to the next, and divided into three parts. Thus, from one birthday to the next, you experience three four-month cycles.

The number of a four-month cycle delineates the predominating influence in your life during that particular third of a year. To find this influence, whether it will be circumstantial, emotional, or mental, you derive the ruling number first, and then consult its interpretation below.

How To Get the Number of Your Four-Month Cycles

You must keep in mind that there are three four-month cycles between your birthdays. For example, if you were born on February 22, 1900, your first four-

81

month cycle would last from February 22 to June 22; your second four-month cycle would last from June 23 to October 22; your third four-month cycle would last from October 23 to February 22 — your next birthday. The number of each of these four-month cycles is derived in a different way, and the explanation for finding each follows.

First Four-Month Cycle of Influence

To get the number of your first four-month cycle, you simply subtract your present age in years from the year of your last birthday; then you reduce the remainder to a single digit. For example: If you were born on February 22, 1900, you would put down the year of your last birthday, assuming that that was in 1944, at which time you were 44 years old. You subtract the 44 from the 1944, and the remainder is 1900. You reduce this to a single digit by adding the numbers together: 1 + 9 = 10; the zeros do not count, and are always dropped, so the remainder is 1. This makes the number of your first four-month cycle — from February 22 to June 22 — a number 1 cycle of influence.

Second Four-Month Cycle of Influence

To get the number of the second 4-month cycle in your individual year, you subtract the number of your Life Cycle from the number of the year of your last birthday. Then you reduce the remainder to a single digit.

In order to compute the Life Cycle Number, you simply add together the number value of the month, day, and year you were born; then reduce this to a single digit. For example: If you were born on February 22, 1900, you would add the number values of this date together, thus: $2 + 2 + 1 + 9 + 0 + 0 = 16$. Then take the total, 16, thus: $1 + 6$ equals 7. This is your Life Cycle number, which you now subtract from the year of your last birthday; let us assume that was in 1944. Thus, 1944 minus 7 equals 1937. You now reduce this to a single digit: $1 + 9 + 3 + 7 = 20$. Zero has no value, so drop it. The result is 2, which is the number of your second four-month cycle of influence, which lasts from June 23 to October 22.

Third Four-Month Cycle of Influence

To get the number of the third four-month cycle, you simply add the numbers of the first two four-month cycles together; then reduce the total to a single digit.

For example: In the above instances, you have 1 for the first and 7 for the second four-month cycle; add them together; the sum is eight, which is the number of your third four-month cycle in this example, lasting from October 23 to February 22.

You have now computed the three numbers of the three four-month cycles between your last birthday and your next one. The meaning of each of these cycles, according to its number, is given in the following paragraphs.

No. 1 Four-Month Cycle

Influences in this cycle are likely to be beneficial. This should be a period of the highest expression of your ambition. The preparation for the fulfillment of your desires should be finished by now and, in this period, you may experience the actual attainment of what you have planned. Your association with men, employers, government officials, fathers, sons, and brothers can be both profitable and mutually enjoyable.

The distinct positive advantages offered to you in this cycle are many. For the first time in a long while, perhaps, your ability to make progress may be enhanced. Leadership and captaincy and forward strides are within easy reach if you will take the first step forward. The presidency of a club, the assumption of authority in an organization, or becoming the main figure in the home may be signified by this cycle.

No. 2 Four-Month Cycle

The vibrancy of the number 2 during this cycle gives you an unparalleled opportunity to express your adaptability. Cooperation, coordination, collaboration, and partnership are the influences indicated. You may succeed in any project which has been started by another person. Your role is that of the practical worker who carries out the design or blue-print of the inventor.

The influence of women may be strongly felt. Associations with women are most likely emphasized as you progress through this cycle. Your attitude here can make this pleasant and beneficial if you concentrate on it. Inspiration may be very stimulating to the mentality. Creative imagination is active; and your efforts in the direction of making things, inventing, or creating should be well rewarded.

No. 3 Four-Month Cycle

This may be considered a period of success provided you don't squander your talents and abilities. The 3 vibration is very strong, and the influences it brings to bear are powerful. You will probably deal with large groups of people, in organizations, clubs, a corporation, or even a group in the service of the country. Your best expression comes through this contact with humanity on a large scale.

The financial influence is also marked, but you must guard all your assets because you will have the desire to play, and you might use up your resources. Good cheer and a happy outlook are yours for the asking during this time, and you can make others happy with very little effort. Social popularity stands out as a strong influence. You may be barraged with invitations and other expressions of affection.

No. 4 Four-Month Cycle

This cycle may seem a little hard to take because its nature is restrictive. The reason is that the four-cycle is one of building and, consequently, of a busy-ness that does not leave much time for pleasure. However, it is just like putting money in the bank — a form of self-denial now for greater future benefits.

Work with a will during this period, for it is part of a plan that is like growing pains: what hurts now will make a bigger, better person of you. The home and the place of work come to the foreground of your attention, and their influence you may not be able to avoid.

Mercy, tolerance, and sympathy are the traits that you can make flourish in your nature now and, as the world needs these so much, you can develop them to the full.

No. 5 Four-Month Cycle

This cycle symbolizes the law of gathering new experiences. The greatest influence here is change. You may travel and thus gather in impressions of a lasting and impressive nature.

New friends are often made in this period, and you should be on the look-out for any interesting new relationship that may arise. Church work and ritual also bear a strong influence in this cycle, and afford much spiritual pleasure.

Salesmanship, research, talk, writing, discussion, and all material affairs are influences of pronounced character for these four months. You can succeed in all these fields by application.

You must beware of haste and speed, however, for the 5 loves action, even of the destructive type.

No. 6 Four-Month Cycle

The number 6 cycle symbolizes the material law of supply. During this period you can receive money and material supplies if you make an effort. It is true that you may be required to share some of this supply or goods, for one influence of the 6 is responsibility. However, all your needs can be fulfilled by your attempts to gain and a willingness to share with others.

During this period another powerful influence is education. You may learn things of priceless value, whether through formal education or experience. Married life and romance are under the reign of the 6 cycle, and these influences will also affect you.

Harmony, rhythm, beauty, and culture are influences of lasting quality of which you may take full advantage for the duration of this cycle.

No. 7 Four-Month Cycle

Intellectual pursuits are the main influences during this cycle. The quiet pleasures of the mind will be more likely to appeal to you than less refined entertainment. This is an excellent period in which to develop the mind as well as to pursue studies of a mystic nature.

Composers and inventors flourish during these cycles so, if you have any ideas, this is the time to seek to put them to practical application.

Affairs which concern people with whom you need to communicate may be carried to a successful conclusion now. You can carry out plans concerning matters in which a personal contact is unnecessary or impractical.

There is a negative aspect of the 7 cycle to watch out for. Because the 7 is slow by nature, delays may cause you disappointment; therefore, be punctual in all you do.

No. 8 Four-Month Cycle

You may express power to the fullest during this period. The magnet of the 8 is at your service; all you need do is avail yourself of what is at hand for you. Force and energy are at your comand to do with what you will.

Executive ability is the strong influence of this cycle. You can now take the reins and direct the traffic of your desires. In material affairs and in relations with other people, you may decide the direction of your will.

Endurance is another influence you will most likely feel. However, and fortunately, discrimination is yours, so that you will understand the power that has been entrusted to you. On your way up, therefore, don't forget to be kind to those who helped you on other levels.

No. 9 Four-Month Cycle

Since 9 is the all-inclusive number, which cancels itself out in all mathematical calculations, it as a universal influence in this cycle. It gives off the influences of balance, growth, and gain. During this cycle you may cast off the old modes and ways that have deterred you up to the present time. Take all partings cheerfully; you must make way for the new.

You may succeed in all affairs dealing with humanitarian societies or activities. The best way to use the 9 cycle to your own advantage is to render service to others. By expressing this high ideal, you will bring all the influences of good to bear on your side.

Say a cheerful farewell to all the negative influences of the pattern of your life. Use the 9 cycle to prepare yourself for the adventure and the glory of the coming new experiences.

Must quit smoking in order to clear my lungs. That's what my subconscious is telling me in order that I might not burn in this life.

Chapter X

THE NUMBER VALUE OF THE LETTERS OF THE ALPHABET

Occult tradition holds that the first sound uttered by man was "Oom." This is the sound vibration still used in the East in the practice of Yoga when the breath is expelled from the lungs through the nostrils. It is doubtless the same vibration as the Western "I am" which is intoned by occidental practitioners of Yoga.

Every letter of the alphabet has a vibratory equivalent in number. The cabala was written in Hebrew, which is a phonetic language, so each *sound* had a numerical equivalent. English has a different alphabet, and it is not a phonetic language, so the numerical equivalent of its letters differs from the ancient cabalistic values.

In the accompanying chart, the number value of every letter is given for the current English alphabet.

Each letter of the alphabet is the symbol of a concept and has its own numerical value. These are fully explained in the alphabet given below.

Does every word have its own vibration? Yes!

How is the number vibration computed? Write out the word; put the number value of the vowels above them, and the number value of the consonants below them. Add the totals of the vowels and consonants separately, so you have the "vowel vibrations" and the "consonant vibrations" separately, and compute their total value by adding these two sub-totals together, and reducing to a single digit.

Single Number Value
of each letter

Letter			Value
a	j	s	1
b	k	t	2
c	l	u	3
d	m	v	4
e	n	w	5
f	o	x	6
g	p	y	7
h	q	z	8
i	r		9

For example:

```
5   9      vowel vibration equal . . . . . . . . . . . . . 14
d e v i l
4   4   3  consonant vibrations equal . . . . . . . . . 11
                                               _____
                                    Total . . . . 25
```

Reduced to a single digit, 2 plus 5 equals 7, total vibration.

Another example shows the difference in the vibration of words, where one letter is omitted:

```
5   9      vowel vibrations equal . . . . . . . . . . . . . . 14
e v i l
4   3      consonant vibrations equal . . . . . . . . . . . 7
                                               _____
                                    Total . . . . 21
```

Reduced to a single digit, 2 plus 1 equals 3, total vibration.

Every word, thus, tells a story when you know the meaning of each letter which comprises it. This is particularly important when you want to interpret your name. All your characteristics, qualities, and hidden traits are revealed by your name. The vowels tell your innate traits, the consonants those you are trying to express, and the total of the two tell what impression you are making on the world.

Because these three phases or aspects of your name are so vitally important, a separate chapter is devoted to the significance of each. However, the "long story" of the revelations made by your name is contained in the individual letters which comprise it. For this reason, the meaning of every letter of the alphabet is given here.

For the full understanding of a name, study every letter in it. Begin with the first letter, read its meaning; go on to the second; and so on. After you have made this interesting investigation, total the number values of the vowels, consonants, and their total when added together. All this is fully explained in the next three chapters.

Here you are given the alphabet, the single and full numerical value of each letter, its symbolism, and its interpretation.

A — No. 1. The letter A is the first in the English alphabet. It is the symbol of man standing upright, and thus denotes initiative and leadership. Creative talents and originality are denoted by this letter. If A is the first letter in your name, it signifies that you have a strong will, determination, and an aggressive personality. If A is the first vowel in your name (following a consonant), it denotes that you have a domineering nature. The A repeated frequently in a name gives the bearer a love of adventure and great stick-to-itiveness. Activity, productiveness, and travel are part of the letter A's significance.

B — No. 2. The letter B symbolizes the life-force or spirit, being poured into the empty vessel, or the body. As the first letter in your name, it denotes an emotional nature. It always signifies willingness to cooperate, the traits required in a partner or collaborator, the ability to obey orders and to carry out instructions faithfully and "to the letter." As the first consonant in your name, following a vowel, it signifies an introspective nature, and endows you with keenly analytical abilities to understand both yourself and others. In life's drama, you will be the builder rather than the architect if there are many B's in your name.

C — No. 3.   The letter C signifies your intellectual qualities and potentialities in the creative field. It stands for the self-expression of very personal ideas. In your name, it has a vitalizing force, and tends to produce a splendid outlook physically and mentally. If C is the first consonant in your name, it signifies an optimistic nature and a happy emotional life. This letter is symbolic of destiny, for that is the function of its numerological equivalent, the 3; when it is repeated often in the name, it denotes your having to learn your Karmic lessons well — and they tend to make you reach your goal and achieve success only after you have overcome many obstacles.

D — No. 4.   The letter D is one completely enclosed, just like its geometrical symbol, the square. You are represented within this enclosure if the first letter in your name is D, or if this letter is repeated frequently in your name. The force of this symbol is that you must rise above adversity, and forget that you are bounded by material barriers. Restrictions and limitations may seem an unduly severe burden if this letter occurs many times in your name, but you still have the noble potentiality of rising above its limitations, and thus becoming an advanced and developed human being, with justice, tolerance, and equity as your ideals in life.

E — No. 5.   The letter E is intellectual or mental in character. It is the letter of letters, bringing to the fore the use of words, the voice, and all forms of communication. The letter E is like a catalytic agent; it activates everything with which it comes in contact. It produces energy and excitement. As the first letter or first vowel in your name, it gives you marked ability to act, preach, broadcast, write, sing, and so on down the list of things done with words. If it is repeated often in the name, it indicates doing this type of work before the public, and acquiring fame through one of these branches of art. The letter E is the courier of the alphabet, winging words on the atmosphere.

F — No. 6. The letter F is the symbol of domestic felicity, denoting the physical care of the home and family. It is the letter of the law of protection, particularly of children and of older relatives. As the first letter or the first consonant in your name, it denotes your willingness to assume the responsibilities in life that are assigned to adults with a grown-up point of view and psychology. If the letter F recurs frequently in your name, it is an indication of the protection of your material affairs with, however, duties and tasks that might be costly. This letter is upright and the support or pillar of the name in which it occurs, as, for example, fairness, father, fidelity.

G — No. 7. The letter G turns in upon itself, signifying an introspective nature which is concerned with the self. It denotes self-study, and the art of meditation. As the first letter, or the first consonant, in your name, the letter G denotes a desire not only to understand yourself, but the world you live in. You are a clever analyst if this letter occurs in your name frequently. You can get to the bottom of events and character, and you understand the motives from which people function. There is a mystic depth to your nature, and you have a keen intuition that is tantamount to well-developed psychic powers. With the guidance provided by this quality, you should advance far in life.

H — No. 8. The letter H is symbolized by a ladder,

which it resembles in appearance. Of course, this indicates two directions — up and down. If this is the first letter in your name, it signifies that you have the choice within you of rising or descending the scale of life. You have strong potentialities for material progress, and you have just as strong possibilities of making errors on the material plane. The same is true of the development of your character. You can become a developed soul, or you can sink to lower spiritual depths. The power is there in the magnet of your personality; it depends upon you to make the proper choice for your own growth, beauty, and happiness.

I — No. 9. The letter I is like the number 9, universally inclusive. The 9 cancels itself out in combination with any other number; the "I" of the personality is a small universe in itself. The symbol of the I is a column or pillar, upright, indestructible, standing through the ages. This letter is the last of those equivalent to single digits (all the ones following being "double numbers"), and thus symbolizes the closing of a cycle. As the first letter in your name, or as the first vowel, the I denotes psychic powers, universal tolerance and sympathy, and time spent on the welfare of others. Repeated often in your name the I indicates extreme sensitivity, and hence possible suffering. It also denotes travel and communication with people long distances away.

J — No. 10. (single value — 1). Leadership is yours if you have J as the first consonant in your name, or if it appears therein frequently. It also denotes an elevated station in life, for it has all the power of Number 1 magnifed ten times by being followed by the cipher or zero. Gain is indicated by this letter, and such profit is likely to come from a new idea, a new concept, or an original invention. The J is intellectual in character, and denotes, in the name, the pursuit of cultural activities. The letter J in your name gives you a magnetic and brilliant personality.

K — No. 11 (single value — 2).   The letter K in a name gives the bearer thereof a vivid, magnetic, and electric individuality. The number 11 doubles all the strength of forceful number 1, and in addition has the sensitive and cooperative vibrancy of the number 2, its form as a single digit. Strength and endurance are yours when this letter appears in your name. If it is the first consonant in your name, it denotes a sunny disposition combined with martial potentialities. It bequeathes upon the bearer, when it appears as the first consonant in a name, a dramatic quality and a love of the theatre and all forms of entertainment and public enterprise.

L — No. 12 (single value — 3).   The letter L is one of beauty of character and of sound. As the first consonant in your name, or as a letter repeated often therein, it denotes success, social popularity, and versatality. The letter L also signifies a highly developed intuition upon which you can depend in times of need. It gives you a keen insight into the motives of other people, so that you understand why they act as they do. It is also the guardian of your individuality, for it reveals to you, in your first impressions, what kind of people and situations you are dealing with. Much movement is indicated by this letter, and a very active life for the one in whose name it appears. The emotional life of the person in whose name the L recurs often is full, romantic and quixotic.

M — No. 13 (single value — 4).   The letter M possesses strength of character in concentrated form. Like its physical shape, it stands firmly upon its own two feet. It denotes cumulative and concentrative powers, the ability to study, and an orderly mind. This letter is the mason of the alphabet; it builds story upon story in its efforts to reach the highest of human aspirations — heavenly enlightenment for the soul and spirit. When this letter occurs as the first consonant in a name, it signifies work, love of harmony in the home, and a nature imbued with the noblest of ideals. If often repeated in a name, the letter M indicates determination and grit that will never accept defeat or ignominy.

N — No. 14 (single value — 5). The letter N has magnetic qualities. It is like a radio receiving set that picks up ideas, concepts, and sound vibrations right out of the ether. In popular parlance, it never misses a trick. Always on the alert, the N seems to reach right out to the best thing, and attract it to itself. It is intellectually inconsistent, in that it will discard as much as it takes in if it cannot progress or advance by its intake. As the first letter in your name, or the first consonant, it will endow you with fluidity, a mercurial nature, and a tendency to scatter many of your talents. The influence of the N is to endow the mind with the spark of divine imagination.

O — No. 15 (single value — 6). The letter O is, as its shape reveals, a symbol of the cosmos. It is the equivalent of the egg of theosophy, the universe in microcosm. As such, it stands for the law of material responsibility. It is the lower plane of the occult aphorism, "As above, so below," for all that is taking place on the astral plane takes place here under the rulership of the O and its numerological equivalent, the 6. In

your name, the O endows you with intellectuality, balance, and the ability to handle your problems. The
home, business, children, and affection are under the
aegis of this letter, and these become the main points
of interest in your life. It circumscribes your life and
career within the circle that it forms, but it allows of
upward, spiritual growth. It is, in truth, the magic
circle, for as it encloses, so also it releases.

P — No. 16 (single value — 7). The letter P is best
understood by a word of which it is the first consonant:
precaution. It is the symbol of the law of preservation.
As the first letter, or the first consonant in your name,
it indicates clarity of mental vision and foresight. It
denotes intellectual qualities, mental curiosity, and a
deep interest in the ego and its development. Power
and success follow in the wake of him whose name
bears many P's, but it requires caution to retain the
heights to which he wins. The study of mystic philosophy is counseled to those whose names are heavy with
the frequency of this letter, for its vibration is potent
for both good and evil, and the balance in favor of
the good must be sought through meditation and
concentration.

Q — No. 17 (single value — 8). The letter Q vibrates to the frequencies of the 1 and the 7; this dual-
ity gives it both a forceful and martial quality which is
tempered by mysticism. As a physical symbol, it is the O
with something added, and that something is a new dimension which releases some of the restrictive quality
of the O alone. It is like the wing on the plane, which
gives the power to rise, to attain great heights, particularly in the spiritual world, if the interest is centered
therein but, strangely, also on the material plane where

great financial success can be attained if you have this letter in your name — in any position. The letter Q in a name has almost mystic qualities as an attention-getting device, and endows its bearer with potent magnetism.

R — No. 18 (single value — 9). The letter R has extremely powerful vibrations. These are of such potency that they endow you with high voltage if this letter appears often in your name. As the first letter or first consonant in your name, it denotes occult potentialities with destructive forces. Like electricity, it can be used for constructive or destructive effects, and this is the lesson of the person whose name bears the letter R, that he must learn the law of discrimination. He is at the switch of tremendous forces, and must know when to use them for eliminating, when for building.

S — No. 19 (single value—1). The letter S symbolizes the rising sun of a new dispensation. It is the equivalent of the Wheel of Fortune, denoting the beginning of a new cycle. The combination of number 1 and number 9 — the two extremes of the single digits — indicates man's striving toward his highest aspirations. The S in your name denotes a strong creative impulse which is related to intangible things. The letter S is an incentive to strong ideas and indicates a new start along spiritual lines. If it recurs frequently, it may indicate emotional involvement during cycles when its influence is strong. Its physical appearance resembles the serpent — theosophical symbol of occult mysteries reserved to the hierachy of initiates.

T — No. 20 (single value — 2). The letter T is the symbol of the cross. It denotes the highest effort put forth for the cause of humanity. Reduced to terms of everyday living, it stands for all the cooperation signified by number 2 and intensified ten times by being followed by the zero. As the first letter in your name or the first consonant, it denotes a nature whose stress is toward the feminine principle of building upon the foundation laid by another — of following rather than leading. It signifies plasticity of character and indicates indecision at vitally important crises. T is the letter of devotion. Bear in mind, "It is more blessed to give than to receive."

U — 21 (single value — 3). The letter U is the symbol of the cup in the Tarot, an open vessel into which are poured the gifts of imagination, charm, inspiration, and romance. As the first vowel in your name, or repeated often, it denotes that you will receive many benefits from life. But the vessel is open, and the gifts may pour over the sides and out — if you are not careful to retain the balance needed. This letter has a refining effect upon those who come under its influence. It is like Maya, or illusion; the fairy gifts of the Tarot are lent for a specific purpose, and when that purpose is achieved, the gifts are liable to vanish back into thin air. It denotes popularity, pleasure, and success, and the scattering of the harvest of the years.

V — No. 22 (single value — 4). The letter V combines the virtues of number 4 and two 2's. It gives the desire and ability to study advanced metaphysics to those in whose name it appears. It denotes hard work but also gratifying rewards therefore. Under the influence of the V vibration, theory is put into practice and, on a higher level, the Plan of the Master is carried out.

This, in other words, is the letter of demonstration — the demonstration on the earth plane of the designs, plans, and concepts which are seemingly "snatched" from the astral and brought down to earth. With this powerful letter in your name, you bring to practical, visible forms the visions called celestial.

W— No. 23 (single value — 5). The letter stands for change, the conversion from old conditions to new. As change is often surprising in nature, the influence of the W is said to be shocking at times. If you have W in your name, it denotes wavering emotions. It is indicative of the necessity to learn to be dynamic, to flow with the tide, and to eliminate the tendency to support the status quo or static conditions. The repetition of W in a name denotes an acquisitive nature. It endows you with a love of speed, travel, words, excitement, adventure, and all that is dramatic and swiftly moving.

X — No. 24 (single value — 6). The letter X occurs but rarely in English words and names. It is the universal symbol of abnegation. It has the power of "x"-ing out — thus eliminating personality from the compound of the human totality or ego. This letter denotes the law of responsibility on the highest, or spiritual, plane. In a name, it endows the bearer with a strong desire for the amelioration of mankind, for the dictating of the law, and the teaching of the tenets of humanity. Spiritual love is the highest expression of him who bears the letter X in his name.

Y — No. 25 (single value — 7). The symbol of the letter Y is the diviner, the rod with forked tip, which is used for the discovery of oil or water under the surface of the earth. This is a most apt symbol, for the letter Y stands for the search for the esoteric or mystic element of life. When this letter appears in a name, it endows the bearer with the yearning for the secrets of initiation into the doctrine "behind the veil." It is also similar to the period of initiation, for it is a slow vibration, repressed, held back, tentative, and dependent for release from delay on the individual's power to acclimate himself to new conditions by learning, and particularly by earning, through meditation and good deeds, the rewards that the Y has the power to reveal in their secret dwelling place.

Z — No. 26 (single value — 8). The symbol of the letter Z is forked lightning, which it resembles in physical appearance. This describes the potency of the vibration of the letter. It endows you who have this letter in your name with tremendous potentialities, and they may be used for both good and bad. They can destroy when allowed the freedom of their will, and they can build and construct when they are chained to the dams of the will. The force which this letter in your name endows upon you is similar to alternating current. It advances and retreats at the same time. It permits the gain of material wealth, but it takes it away if the wealth is used for selfish ends. It gives political and material power, but removes it if it is abused. You can chain the very elements if you have the vibration of this letter in your name, but it will prove to be a self-destructive force that will destroy you if you do not use it for high spiritual purposes.

Chapter XI

VOWEL VIBRANCY — THE *YOU* THAT YOUR NAME CONCEALS

Every letter in the alphabet has its own number and power of vibration. This number and the meaning thereof is given in full in the preceding chapter, where for the sake of uniformity all the letters have been placed in alphabetical and numerical order.

The vowels and the consonants have different vibrations. Their sounds and the effects thereof differ from each other. For this reason — that they have a different *frequency* — they are treated in separate chapters.

What is the significance of the vowel vibrancy in your name? You do not wear your heart upon your sleeve, but your heart's desire is concealed in the meaning of the vowels of your name. Added together, and reduced to a single digit, the numerical value of the vowels in your name reveals the things your heart really does desire. This vibrancy represents the *you* that you conceal from the world. Your secret ambitions, your hidden likes and dislikes, your personal inclinations, and the longings of your soul are to be found in the analysis of the number of the vowel vibrations in your name. When you are true to the real inner urge of your being, you express this vowel power. But how often does one even know what these desires are? To understand your hidden urges, you should compute the vowel power of your name, and then read the interpretation for that number, which is given below.

How To Compute the Vowel Power in Your Name

To find the vowel power in your name, all you need do is follow the simple instructions herewith:

Write out your name, leaving some space between each letter.

In Chart 2, look up the number value of each vowel.

Write the number value of each vowel above it in your name.

Add these numbers together.

Reduce the total to a single digit.

For Example:

9 + 5 + 5   + 6   equal 25

I R E N E   L O W Y

25 equals 2 + 5 equals 7

7 is the vowel power of the name given.

Now, look up the number 7 below for the meaning of this vowel power vibration in the example given.

Follow the above instructions, using your own name, and look up the meaning of the vowel power of the number you compute from your own name.

Putting the Vowel Power To Work

The vowel power of a name, like the electric current in your power line, has little value if it is not put to work. For this reason, the ways in which you can put to use your knowledge of the vowel power in your name, or anyone else's name, are given here.

You can discover the personal desire or ambition that lies locked in your heart. You can tell how another person will react under all circumstances, for the key to his heart-felt wishes is in your hands.

The marked qualities of your character and of the characters of everyone you wish to analyze will be known to you, and you can thus pre-judge their personal decisions and reactions in crucial moments. Because experience, or the changing of the name, does not alter this vowel vibration of the name given at birth, it is a reliable index, and can be used to avoid unpleasant experiences, misunderstandings, and unhappiness.

Know the nature of the inner urge as revealed by the vowel power before you make such vital decisions as entering business relations, or domestic arrangements, or marriage. With unchanging determination, each individual will seek the expression of his inner urge — consciously or unconsciously. This is a vital secret; it gives him in whose hands it lies cardinal power. Use the power this knowledge gives you for the attainment of your most noble aspirations.

Vowel Vibration No. 1

You have to be at the head of the cosmic parade. Regardless of all your other traits, you wish to lead, to direct, and not to be subordinate. Should you be unable to fulfill your desire in the position or place where life has put you, you will make numerous changes until this gnawing ambition is satisfied. Alone, you display the qualities of courage, strong will, determination, and the ability to overcome powerful adversaries and obstacles. With another, or with more than one, these same traits may devolop into a domineering superiority that makes an unpleasant impression. The urge and the will to lead are potent within you, and they "will out."

Vowel Vibration No. 2

Your instinct is to be friendly, to mix with everyone and to do the little things that others so frequently leave undone. You like to smooth things out and adjust matters when they go wrong. Although you are somewhat inclined to be timid in an argument, you have such a kindly nature that you are rarely put on the spot psychologically. Your desire is for peace — even, perhaps, "peace at any price." You enjoy quiet and the tactics of non-resistance, and you enjoy co-operating with other people. Easily persuaded, you let the willing spirit of your inner self take charge. Diplomacy and tact are highly developed in your character.

Vowel Vibration No. 3

Your inner desire is to find the bright and cheerful side of life. You enjoy good talk, and love to express yourself in words, which seem to hold a fascination for you. You have a vivid imagination, and you like to express your thoughts and fancies in colorful language. You enjoy entertaining your friends, large groups, and the public, for you can express yourself in an artistic manner and in a creative way. You like to exaggerate, for life as you find it is too prosaic for your true taste. You would like to have the means at hand to be generous, kind, even lavish; when circumstances forbid such unselfishness, you may appear to be all wrapped up in yourself — an erroneous impression. You want everyone to be cheerful and happy and, as a natural entertainer, you do a great deal toward this end.

Vowel Vibration No. 4

Your innermost urge is to see a good job well done. You have an inner voice — your conscience — that revolts against anything unfinished or incorrect. You like to see things managed in a practical way, and you make every effort to put everything in its place, and keep it there. You like to see everything just so, and you feel that your practical outlook is a good way of looking at things. You establish routine because you see virtue in its nature and accomplishment in its system. You dislike waste, petty arguments, and the strict interpretation of the law. Because your word is your bond, you feel that everyone else should live up to the highest ethical standard you have set for yourself, in your heart; and you are right!

Vowel Vibration No. 5

Your inner urge is toward distant and romantic places with names that recall the glamour of days of adventure. To you, variety is the very breath of life, and change and motion are the beat of your heart. You seek freedom, and you claim as your cosmic heritage the right of personal thought and action. Details, routine, and schedules dampen your spirits and kill your enthusiasm. To you, monotony is the sin of sins. You are clever and actively interested in pursuits where cleverness spells success. Repartee and wit are the soul of the intellect, in your opinion. You like crowds, motion, and speed. Curiosity is the name of your life work, and versatality the by-line.

Vowel Vibration No. 6

You are possessed of strong humanitarian tendencies. You enjoy doing good, and your ideal is to be of service to others. Love and sympathy are the forms of your expression, and tolerance is the core of your philosophy. While you have the troubles of the world on your mind, and seek a way to solve them, you are also fond of those who are near and dear to you, and you desire their approbation for all you do, both for them and for humanity. Harmony, beauty, and rhythm are as necessary to you as the breath you draw. You have strong artistic urges, and inwardly you yearn for recognition as an artist in some field of endeavor or expression. Beauty, truth, justice, and love are the foundation stones of your heart's desire.

Vowel Vibration No. 7

Your intuition is highly developed, and you probably are aware of your inner urge to study the mystic and mysterious aspects of nature. The hidden forces of the world hold a deep attraction for you, and nothing gives you greater pleasure than the rewards of the study of the psychic phenomena that have been recorded or that you have experienced. You like to observe, to draw conclusions, and to keep the results of your analyses to yourself. You are not selfish, but you are aware of the danger of indulging the idle curiosity of the merely curious. You admire mental courage, intellectual tenacity, and spiritual bravery. This trinity forms the triangle of your own desire.

Vowel Vibration No. 8

You admire success, and it is your inner ambition to achieve it in your chosen field. You have the ability to work long and laboriously, sacrificing everything else in the way of pleasure to the attainment of your goal in life. You desire power, acclaim, and position, because you think these will bring to you the other things you want in life — the best in everything. With you, quality is what really counts. You do not tolerate the tawdry, and you do not bargain for the second-best. You can sway the masses, you can sell, merchandise, and advertise. You can be the great philanthropist or the benevolent despot. Great spiritual power can be yours, too, when you develop your greatest secret urge, which is to advance in the truly advanced departments of life.

Vowel Vibration No. 9

You are the dreamer of dreams. In your secret heart, you have a vision of loveliness for yourself and for the world that is truly celestial in its concept. You are alert to all the finer things of life, and appreciate them not only as a connoisseur, but as a creator. So close to your heart are the ideals you behold with your inner eye, that you suffer miseries at the thought of the harsh realities of life. You would have everything at its peak of artistic production, and you would convert the schedule of the world to that of a place wherein every man and woman attains the greatest of all pleasures — and the one you seek for yourself, the pleasure of doing good and important work, and enjoying it at the same time.

Chapter XII

CONSONANT VIBRATIONS — THE
PASSIVE *YOU*

Each letter in the alphabet has its individual number value and meaning. Because the vowels, consonants, and their total have a significance of their own, the meanings of their total value (reduced to a single digit) are given in separate chapters. You will find below the meanings of the number value of the consonants in your name when they have been reduced to a single digit.

How to find the Consonant Value of Your Name

To find the consonant value of your name, follow these simple directions:

Write out your name, leaving a space between each letter.

Consult Chart 2 for the number value of each consonant.

Write the number value of each consonant under it.

Add these numbers together.

Reduce the total to a single digit.

The number thus arrived at is the consonant vibration of your name.

For Example:

I R E N E   L O W Y
9 + 5   + 3 + 5 + 7   equal 29
2 + 9 equal 11
1 + 1 equal 2

Thus 2 is the consonant vibration of the name in the example.

Find the consonant vibration of your name by following the directions above, and read the interpretation for the number given below.

Putting the Consonant Vibration to Work

Knowing the consonant vibration of your name will will help you to understand yourself.

By computing this number for any other name, you will better understand the person you wish to analyze.

The consonant vibration represents you in your passive moods. It shows what you are when you are not acting or reacting.

People are like chemical elements; alone, they have traits of their own. In the company of one person, they act differently. In a group, their conduct takes on still another pattern. That is the effect of number!

What are you like when you are alone? The answer is in the consonant vibration of your given name at birth.

Consonant Vibrancy No. 1

You believe there must be a worthwhile purpose in everything you do. Without a definite program, or aim, you are unenthusiastic and uninspired. Strong will power characterizes you, and ambition is the driving force which propels you forward. You like to have your every wish gratified, and sometimes you rationalize your self-indulgence as a form of duty.

The passive you may be ruled by passion, and your attitude may be domineering. To attain your ends, you may act from selfish motives. Improvement can come by developing altruism, noble ideals, and spiritual aspirations.

Consonant Vibrancy No. 2

You are a builder, visualizing enchanted castles in material form. The use of charm is at your disposal, and you succeed in getting much of what you want because others wish to please you. You have faith in the universal laws which bring reward to the good and punishment to the evil.

The passive you may be destructive if you do not get your way. Deliberate cunning may be conceived in your mind, and scheming actions result from the frustration of your wishes. Your natural inclination is to help others, and the greatest help you can be to yourself is to follow your natural inclinations.

Consonant Vibrancy No. 3

You have faith in the future, are filled with hopefulness, and do not require constant reassurances to face the things to come. In you there is a voice that tells you that your destiny will be fulfilled and that the purpose of your life will be achieved regardless of present circumstances.

The passive you may take another path, that of non-resistance. You may feel that life has battered you so much that no effort is worth while. Improvement can be made by acting with great courage. Express your talent; have no fear; and be free!

Consonant Vibrancy No. 4

You have stability and balance which make you very self-reliant. It is not necessary for you to seek outside amusements, for you are very good company for yourself. Power and strength make you the stand-by of your own needs as well as the needs of your friends. You have ability, and you use it to worthy ends and gains.

The passive you may see hardship in things where it does not really exist. You may play the role of the slave-driver all too realistically, though unconsciously. Meet your deficiencies by obeying the clarion call of your indomitable will.

Consonant Vibrancy No. 5

You fearlessly swing through life, seeking adventure, careless of the morrow, and carefree in your heart. Happiness comes to you from your very soul, for it is your cosmic legacy that this be so. You do not build for the future, nor of the bricks and mortar of permanence, but for present joy. You look upward, never down. You are imaginative and mystical, and your role is that of dreamer and magician.

Although you could be a sorcerer, do not indulge your fancy thus. Fasten your thoughts and acts on self-development rather than the development of charlatanry, for within you are wells of power and graciousness.

Consonant Vibrancy No. 6

You enjoy the peace of solitude that is described in Holy Writ when you are told to "Go into thy closet, and pray, and that that thou askest shall be granted thee." Harmony is yours because you have confidence in attaining your desires.

You know that the abundance of natural good will can never be exhausted, and so your personal slogan is that all is well. Luxury is not necessary to your happiness, but comfort and balance are. Ease of your disappointment comes from the inner well of your wisdom, patience, and faith.

Consonant Vibrancy No. 7

When you are alone, you are at peace with the world. Quiet, solitude, and relaxation are natural to you. You know how to be still, and in contemplation you find rest for the soul. You are languorous in your habits and subtle in your thinking. The unexpected holds little surprise for you, for your attitude is one prepared for anything.

Your outlook is one of faith based on intelligent action. You can stand alone, and loneliness holds no fears for you. A profound sympathy with the rest of the world stirs you to immortal prayer for the happiness of others and for lasting peace.

Consonant Vibrancy No. 8

Strong protective forces surround you, and you reflect their strength in your mental processes as well as in the conduct of your life. You know how to deal with the material problems that you face, and so you have no complexes on that score. Business affairs hold no qualms for you.

You are happy in solitude because you know how to employ your time to good advantage. Problem solving is a delightful mental pastime for you, and you know how to get along well with yourself.

Consonant Vibrancy No. 9

"The truth, and nothing but the truth" — the ancient oath of the courts of law is the slogan of your life. You are tolerant of everything but that which stands in the way of justice and constructive action. The life force of your whole entity is devoted to the expression of pure spirit.

Conscience is your guide, and inspiration the motivating force of your being. You are absolutely sincere, truthful, noble, vivid, creative, and vital. Your emotions and your intellect are well balanced. Your intuition guides you toward the establishment of perfection.

Chapter XIII

ALL OF YOU — EXPRESSED IN YOUR FULL NAME

You have now delved into the secrets of your personality as revealed by the numbers of the vowels and consonants in your name. These are veritably secrets, for they represent your inmost desires and your silent or passive thoughts and actions.

What are you expressing to the world? The answer to this question lies in the total number derived from the addition of all the letters in your name (reduced to a single digit).

Since you have already computed the number value of the vowels and consonants in your name, all you need do is add them together and reduce the total to a single digit. If you have not done this computation previously, follow the simple directions given herewith.

How To Compute the Number Value of
Your Name in Full

1. Write out your full name.
2. Leave spaces between each letter.
3. Above each vowel, put its number value (see Chart 2).
4. Below each consonant, put its number value (see Chart 2).
5. Add these number values, and then reduce the total to a single digit.

For example:

$$9 + 5 + 5 \quad + 6 \qquad = 25$$
I R E N E   L O W Y
$$9 + 5 \quad + 3 + 5 + 7 = 29$$

Total $= 54$

$$54 = 5 + 4 = 9$$

Thus the number which expresses the total personality of the bearer of this name is 9.

Compute the number of your total personality as revealed by your name, and read the description of what you are expressing as given below.

What Does Your Expression Number Express?

Your free will permits you to change your name whenever you desire. By doing so, you change the expression by which the world knows you.

A moment's reflection will bring enough evidence to your consciousness to demonstrate that there is more to a name than Shakespeare ever dreamed of when he asked, "What's in a name?" for, truly, the answer is, "Everything."

When a woman marries and changes her name, the most frequent cause and method of changing names that is known, she changes everything about her whole life.

When a person embarks upon a public career, he changes his name — and thus changes the vibratory influence or expression he is putting forth. Theatre marquees literally shine with names that the famous have chosen for themselves. Mary Pickford was originally Gladys Smith; Sarah Bernhardt changed her name from Rose Bernard; Cary Grant was born Archie

Leach; Mme. Magda Lupescu was christened Mary Wolf. Choose almost any star of the entertainment world or famous personage, and you will find that he or she changed his or her original name, and thus the career and expression, at some time.

The name you use tells what you are expressing. It is the clue to your mission on earth and is the key number to what you must do for others.

In the Bible, the Creator ascribed a special name to anyone appointed to a special mission. He told Simon that he would henceforth be called Peter, for "on this rock (Peter), shall be built the church."

Thus, your name tells your mission. When your free will alters or changes your mission, you change your name.

It is, however, no "accident" that you were given your particular name at birth. It is a part of the Great Plan. Therefore, you should take into serious consideration any change of name that you contemplate.

The numbers given below tell your purpose in life. Before you make any change in your name to make it come out to a particular number or description which appeals to you, ask yourself whether you are fitted to carry out the mission or purpose that number stands for.

What a No. 1 Full Name Value Expresses

Your purpose in life is to express perfected individuality. The right of the individual to express himself is the keynote of your charter of humanity. As you face life in its day-to-day aspects, you will have to make your own decisions. Not only will you have to play the role of the leader, but you will have to help others to find themselves. Courage distinguishes you, and you will employ it to carry out your original ideas. The world will look to you for strength and force of character. To fail it would be to fail in your mission in life.

When you neglect to live up to your best self, you display the traits of a dictator. Aggression and dominance then manifest themselves. Selfishness and hauteur come to the fore instead of valor and initiative. Your aim then becomes diverted from the group aim to the egotistical aim. Therefore, the energy which is produced by the generator of your name vibration should be used for constructive purposes only. Because your greatest asset is your individuality, you should work alone, in your own way, for the best results. You must not only face, but pass, the test of originality and action.

It is truly said that he who hesitates is lost. This lifetime is your opportunity to show what you can accomplish by the force of your free will. Accept nothing at its face value, nor bend the knee to authority or tradition. A noble life can be yours if you follow your natural inclination to assert yourself.

You are the executive; live up to your part!

What a No. 2 Full Name Value Expresses

You express the cooperative spirit. Through your sympathy and good will, you find happiness, for depression will only mark the periods of your life when you permit a lack of harmony to exist. The key to your success is in winning your way, not forcing it. You delight in group and community projects, in bringing people together, and in tactfully straightening out knotty situations.

Because you have such a diplomatic nature, you are able to meet people of all classes and stations in life. You feel at ease everywhere, and you know just how to put others at their ease. Your role is that of the cosmic peace-maker. Your expression, pattern of life, mission, and duty is to help establish peace. You calm the troubled waters of life and dwell in serenity because of your calm and settling influence.

When you fail to express your true self, you act conceited and ignorant. People get the impression that you are suavely hypocritical, yet try to use you for all you're worth. Your reaction may be to become secretive and petty, full of self-pity for the abuse you really brought upon yourself. Then you emphasize the past and avidly hoard possessions.

Expressing your best self means being agreeable and sincere. You are known to be genuine, and you have a reputation for being gallant. Because you have keen insight into the feelings of others, you act with sympathy. You are sensitive and intuitive and not only ferret out the secrets of others, but soothe their ruffled feelings. You are life's diplomat, and the world is your "portfolio."

What a No. 3 Full Name Value Expresses

To inspire and uplift others is the form of expression carved out for you by destiny. The need of your soul is for the full and complete expression of all that is bright, gay, and optimistic in life. You are a natural gloom-chaser, dispensing cheer wherever you go. Because you can liquidate negative thoughts and moods, you are looked to for relief from depression and protection from melancholy. Your inherent expression originates in your creative and artistic ability which makes it possible for you to see the beauty in life and point it out to others. Only in your generous giving of yourself to others do you find real happiness, for the secret of experience is yours: that service brings joy.

Words and actions are the happy medium of the natural expression of your own ideas. Through these media, you fulfill your expression and work out life's lesson. You are able to create in an artistic way, and your strong imagination produces brilliant concepts. Charm distinguishes you, and wit marks your conversation. You take the popularity which is yours with easy grace.

When you disregard your better instincts and the dictates of the inner voice, you scatter your talents and fritter your time away. Like a butterfly, you flit from one pursuit to another, idly, and without climax or accomplishment. Then you talk too much, go in for lavish adornment and uncontrollable passions.

You have a glorious mission in life — to reveal the beauty of the earth, nature, philosophy, and life itself to the unenlightened. Grasp the noble opportunity before you to teach others to see, and your own vision, perception, insight, and hidden powers will increase to your lasting happiness.

What a No. 4 Full Name Value Expresses

Your purpose in life is to build. Block by block, the construction of your own career, your happiness, and a life work of value to the society in which you live, is the object of your whole existence. The symbol of your expression is the square; and four-square is the synonym of honesty which is not only your policy and slogan, but the ideal which you desire to see built into the minds of men and the structure of society. You are straightforward in all your dealings, and you also bear the responsibility of maintaining equity as the code of ethics and conduct for people in general. Your life work is built upon a foundation of service, and the structure which rises from it is one devoted to the betterment of mankind. There may not be much wandering in romantic glades or glamorous ports of call for you, for your work is always at hand.

When you rebel against the seeming restrictions of your life, you are only making it difficult for yourself. The only way to meet the service which it is your destiny to perform, is with the realization that your calling is noble and that none other is higher. At such times you will work hard, but it will be to no avail. Worry and penury will make you disagreeable, and your tasks will seem to increase in number and ardor, with no rest or vacation from your labors. Jealousy, pettiness, and narrow views will limit your mental and emotional horizons. On the other hand, by meeting your destiny with a smile, you can attain the highest peaks of accomplishment, enjoy the thrill of your constructive efforts and, from the top of the edifice of your achievements, view the world in peace, contentment, and the satisfaction that rewards good deeds well done.

What a No. 5 Full Name Value Expresses

Change, novelty, and progress mark your career.

Your expression takes the form of vocal aptitude, oratory, writing, broadcasting, and all the arts which spread to the world the ideas that spring from your creative imagination. It is said of old that "In the beginning was the word"; it is your purpose in life to spread the word — the word that will release men from bondage, that will cause revolution. This revolution is the turning of the wheel of progress so that the ends of tolerance, freedom, peace, and prosperity to all will be reached. Before your goal is attained, you will have many experiences, and you will travel to many places, and your opinions and concepts will take many forms and assume a variety of shapes. When you have learned that change means progress, you will overcome the uncertainty that accompanies you through this variety of experiences, and will fulfill your purpose in life.

It is not your role in life to be grasping, or to hold on to possessions or attachments. Many times, you will find that you are attempting to cling to things that should be put away or put behind you, only to realize that you can further yourself by letting go. By learning to meet the unexpected with equanimity, by appreciating the fact that change means putting the past into the limbo without regrets, you can work for enduring freedom for yourself and others in whom you can indoctrinate this philosophy. Your destiny is to move with the times. Struggling against your destiny would only bring out the show of your temper, the display of your passions and violence, and would make you wasteful, impulsive, and disagreeable in a vociferous way. Adaptability is your distinguishing trait, and you should employ it to reach your goal —

to become the cosmic orator who helps to free the world.

What A No. 6 Full Name Value Expresses

Your Life purpose is to express some of the highest ideals of humanity. Many responsibilities are yours, for you are the protector of the hearth and home. You are the personification of the moat and armor which ward off enmity, want, and suffering. It is your duty to show the right way to the members of your family and to extend this form of service to humanity. In the broadest sense, this means that you stand for truth and justice. The Golden Rule comprises your code of ethics; you not only live up to it, but you seek to make it the principle of the pattern of life in general. The rule operates accordingly to universal law. Each good you do is like a deposit in a world bank. You do not necessarily get your dividends from the individual whom you help, but from the general good stored up. For this reason benefits come to you from surprising and unexpected sources.

The fine things of life are your delight, and you enjoy them as a connoisseur and a creator. Harmony and beauty are necessary to your happiness, and you are a strong influence in establishing them in every environment where you abide. Your expression is serence except when you by-pass the philosophy of life you know to be the right one. Then you become egocentric, selfish, nagging, crafty, and worrisome; you try to reform the world and rivet unwanted attention on others. Because you are a flame of inspiration when you express the true side of your nature, you should never allow the negative forces of life to influence your conduct. Music, art, and poetry are always a source of solace and inspiration to you. The rhythm of your life can be smooth and cadent, and you should enjoy the beauty your mind and eye behold.

What A No. 7 Full Name Value Expresses

The expression of your name is the symbol of the law of discrimination. You must learn the difference between real, lasting values, and unreal, evanescent evaluations. Many trials and tests must be passed before you come to the realization of your high purpose in life. Appearances can be deceiving, and you must develop your analytical faculties to know the why and wherefore of every experience. Eventually you evolve as an understanding, tolerant, and sympathetic individual with a great heart and a noble soul. The secrets of the universe may be opened to you, for the potentialities for mystic initiation are great within you. Silence and meditation are the media for your development. Paradoxical as it may seem, your "expression" is through silence. Devotion, study, prayer, and meditation are the paths to your development. Nothing is beyond your comprehension once you learn the secret of penetrating the soul of events and people.

You have duties to perform as a healer of bodies and souls. Your work requires a study of the philosophy of occultism, for it will open your eyes to the inner workings of the minds of men. You may be the adornment of a pulpit, but more likely your religion is spiritual, with the heart as its temple and virtue its god.

You may have many obstacles to overcome and many diffculties to vanquish. Your determination to develop and evolve will, however, pay the highest of dividends. Innate sympathy, real beauty of soul, and a sensitive nature distinguish you. The harsh realities of life will not be abrasive to your fine qualities if you guard them within the confines of your eternal spirit.

What A No. 8 Full Name Value Expesses

The expression of your name is one of power, organization, and success. It denotes that you have strengthened the bonds of financial capability, organizational talent, and humanitarian ideals. Truths of universal appeal are known to you, and you operate from a code of the highest aspirations. It is your belief that everyone should share the good in the world from its material and spiritual storehouses. You can acquire money and position by making the effort to do so, and you wisely share your gains with those you love as well as those who are in need. In charitable, philanthropic, and religious movements, you may be the guiding light of inspiration or the administrator of practical affairs. Your role is that of the cosmic magistrate. You will be called upon to judge, and others will abide by your opinions.

Destructive powers of a violent nature are the undeveloped side of your expression. When you neglect the high destiny intended for you, or desert your ideals, you are the cause of unhappiness — your own included. You torment yourself with unfulfilled desires — wealth, and power. Failure discourages you, and discouragement leads to the wilful destruction of your achievements, talents, and peace of mind. Serenity, comfort, and splendid works can all be yours. Devotion to your true aspirations, abiding by your naturally optimistic philosophy, and self-study are the keys to the freedom of the individuality. The power of refusal is great indeed. Accept the high position that has been destined for you. By living as a great person, you can be great indeed.

What a No. 9 Full Name Value Expresses

The expression of your name denotes that your object in life is to attain the divine quality of compassion. Love, tolerance, and service are the trinity of your soul's ambition. You never condemn because all things are negated by your make-up. Your number, 9, is self-effacing. It cancels itself out whenever added to another number or element. So in your expression, the personal elements of envy, jealousy, derision, and condemnation never enter, for they are all eliminated by the pity which fill your heart.

Your expression may seem a heavy cross for you to bear, but only if you see the undeveloped side of the powerful 9 of your name. Disregarding your mission in life may lead to a career of disappointments, solitude, depression, and unhappiness. Love must be the ruler of your life, and its synonym must be service. Remember, when you face unwanted but necessary sacrifices, the words, "He so loved the world." Good works will then flow from you as from a spring whose source is never dry. Love will so encompass you that lonelinesss and unhappiness can never assail you.

Philanthropy, medicine, social service, spiritual leadership, and occult mastery are within the all-embracing ken of the number 9 of your expression. Yours should be a life of the highest attainments on the earth plane; yours it is to make it so!

Chapter XIV
HOW TO GET ALONG WITH
OTHER PEOPLE

Have you ever wondered why you get along with some people and not with others? At a party, do you know why you have an immediate feeling of warmth toward one guest and antipathy toward another? Numerology answers these questions that arise in your daily life. For example, haven't you caught yourself or one of your friends saying, "This is one of my bad days"? How many people have you heard say, "I hate Philadelphia," or, "I love New Orleans?" Yet, isn't a day strictly impersonal? Has a city a soul that can arouse love or hate?

As a matter of fact, every city has a personality all its own, and its personality is reflected in the number derived from letters which make up its name. You respond to the number vibrations of everything that has a name. And numerology explains the vibrations of numbers and letters to which you react.

For example, if your Life Cycle Number is 3, and that of the other person is 6, look up Chart 3; look down the left hand column for No. 6; to the right of the number 6, you will find the guide for your getting along with this number 6 person.

The Compatibility of Names

The single digit to which the numbers in your name are reducible is called your Name Expression Number. To find this number, if you have not already done so, refer to Chapter XIII. To make use of this number in daily life in order to get along with other people, compute the Name Expression Number of the other person; add it to your own; then reduce the sum to a single digit.

The number thus computed will be found at the left of the following chart in the first, or left-hand, column. This number is the "clue" to what you and the other person can express together in perfect compatibility. The forms of expression in which this relationship will succeed are then to be found in column two, at the right of the "clue" number.

For example, if your name is Jane Brown, and you want to find out how to get along with a person named Joe Boyle, compute both your Expression Numbers as follows:

Your name:

$$1 + 5 \quad + 6 \quad = 12 = 1 + 2 = 3$$
$$\text{J A N E} \quad \text{B R O W N}$$
$$1 + 5 + 2 + 9 \quad + 5 + 5 = 27 = 2 + 7 = 9$$

$$\text{Total } 12 = 1 + 2 = 3 \qquad \overline{12}$$

Friend's name:

$$1 \quad + \quad 2 + 7 + 3 \quad = 13 = 1 + 3 = 4$$
$$\text{J O E} \quad \text{B O Y L E}$$
$$6 + 5 \quad + 6 \quad + \quad 5 \quad = 22 = 2 + 2 = 4$$

$$\overline{\text{Total } 8}$$

$$\text{Total } 8 + 3 = 11 = 1 + 1 = 2$$

Thus, the number 2 is the combined vibration of both your names. This number appears in the first column of the following chart. To the right of it, in column 2, you will find the forms of expression which establish compatability between Jane and Joe.

Use this chart for your own "clues" to compatability.

NAME COMPATIBILITY CHART

After you have found the combined vibration of your name and that of another person, you will find the interpretation thereof in the chart below.

Combined Vibration	Forms of Expression Favored
1	Intellectual collaboration, performing duties, government work, organization, club work, starting new projects, invention, hiking, studying, and executive work.
2	Marriage, building personality and charm, erecting a home, cooperation, diplomatic service, cooking, carrying out the plans of other people, helping in the home.
3	Projects dealing with the masses, politics, art, play, entertainment, children, playground work, social pleasures, success in elections, any money-earning project.
4	Hard work projects, corporation work or employment, saving money, gathering resources, building projects, mining projects, farming.
5	Adventure, travel, conversation, making new friends, moving from business or home, sales, research, writing, advertising, radio work, correspondence.
6	Home life, family affairs, comforts, inventions, gadgets, helping others, charitable work, educational projects, money-saving ideas.

7   Cultural pursuits, mystic studies, numerology, musical events, physical exercise, games, sports, tending the sick, planning future projects.

8   Law cases, money earning and saving projects, establishing justice and equity, insurance policies, ocean travel, philanthropic work.

9   Communicating with distant people, occult studies, humanitarian work, friendships, scientific work, investigating or detective activities.

LIFE CYCLE NUMBER CLUES

Your Life Cycle Number is also a clue to your relationship with other people, and you can get along with them compatibly if you know your Life Cycle Number and the Life Cycle Number of the other person. Of course, some people will not give you their birth date as freely as they will give you their name. For this reason, compatability charts are provided for both Name and Birth Date computations. The charts which follow are based upon Life Cycle Numbers for which you have to know the date of birth of the person whose "clue" you wish to look up.

How to use the Life Cycle Compatibilty Charts

To make use of the Life Cycle Compatibility Charts, you must know your Life Cycle Number and that of the person whose "clue" you are seeking. The single digit to which your date of birth is reducible is called your Life Cycle Number. To find this number, if you have not already done so, refer to Chapter III.

Compute the number of the other person in the same way that you compute your own. Then look up the chart headed by the Life Cycle Number that you have arrived at as your own. Look down the left hand column for the number of the person whose clue you are seeking, and to the right, you will find your compatibility guide.

For example, if your Life Cycle Number is 3, and that of the other person is 6, look up Chart 3; look down the left hand column for No. 6; to the right of the number 6, you will find the guide for your getting along with this number 6 person.

Your Life Cycle No. 1 Compatibility Chart

Other Person's Number	GUIDE
1	Each of you has initiative and you can go places together. Perfect coordination can be achieved by heeding each other's advice. Instead of trying to compete with each other, you can each be of invaluable assistance to the other. Don't try to steer the chariot of your relationship, but gracefully listen to the counsel of the other person, and let him or her take the lead, at times, to profit most from this relationship.
2	This relationship should prove of mutual benefit to you and the other person. You have the initiative and original ideas, and the other person has the ability to carry out your ideas and plans. As partners, mates, or

collaborators, you two can become a pair of winners, for each has what the other lacks, and there should be no friction between you.

3   In this relationhip, you have the leadership and originality; the other person has the charm and magnetism to get adherents to your cause so that success seems almost inevitable. As a team, you get along well, with perfect understanding of each other's aims as the basis of almost perfect compatibility.

4   Stay at the helm of this partnership, and all should turn out very well. Your contribution to this relationship is inventiveness, and the other person's contribution is the execution of your plans and schemes. Speed should characterize everything you do together, although you are likely to change your plans often.

5   By letting the other person do the talking, you can get along well in this relationship. Success should come to both of you in domestic and educational projects, as long as you do not interfere with the publicity angles the other person will probably contribute to your partnership.

6   "Take it easy" is the best advice you can follow in trying to get along with the other person. There will be friction if you insist on having your own way. Your best bet is to study cultural subjects or enjoy the arts together. Don't force your ideas.

7 Be moderate in your demands on the other person. You can succeed in money making projects, but that will not necessarily make either of you happy. Together, you express a lot of power. Use it to good ends to really enjoy it.

8 Never let go of your dreams, ideals and aspirations if you would get along well with the other person. Eliminate or avoid friction by not competing with each other. Talk things over before either of you goes ahead on his own. You can go far, but go slowly.

9 You should be the stimulating member of this relationship. Contribute your talents and inventiveness, and accept the sympathy and the prestige that the other person gives to you. Do not let the other person ever discourage you.

Your Life Cycle No. 2 Compatibility Chart

Other Person's Number

GUIDE

1 An excellent combination for success in all mutual projects. You are destined to carry out the plans of the other person, for you have the ability to execute, while the other person has the talent to originate. You can be an inspiration while you also are the personification of cooperation.

2 Perfect equality should exist in this relationship, and each of you should understand the other, work with and for the other, and build a mansion of happiness and friendship with mutual benefits accruing to both parties.

3 To make this partnership a success, you should let the other person lead, while you contribute your social graces and charm to the combination so that you will each enjoy extreme popularity. Remain serene; never show jealousy; do not try to assert yourself, and this combination will last a long time.

4 You will each add strength to the other in the association formed. You are the builder and the other person is the architect of the combination. Together, you can erect a mansion of mutual aid and benefit. Educational matters are strongly favored, as is the home and domestic affairs.

5 Give all your cooperation to this relationship. Let the other person do the talking, appear witty, brilliant, and clever. You can get along excellently if you will take a back seat — except where your stability and fortitude are needed. Don't do anything that might strain the relationship or create friction.

6   This is an excellent combination for material success, earning money, doing charitable work, and also forming corporate organizations. Let the other person take the lead; his ideas are bound to be good, and your work will be to carry them out. The other person willingly assumes obligations; let him or her do so.

7   This is an excellent combination for doing work in the field of psychic research, numerology, and the study of mysticism. You may have to bolster up the morale of the other person very often; accept this chore with grace. Don't get in the other person's way when he wants to be alone.

8   This is a good money combination; you can go far together in attaining material success. You should be able to work out clever plans which add to your prestige and to your reputation. Efficiency should be the by-word of all you do together, and that includes having a good time and enjoying each other's company.

9   Together, you and the other person make a powerful combination. Each adds to the strength and power of the personality of the other. You can lead any cause you choose to espouse. Let the other person use his imagination while you contribute your practicality to the combination.

Your Life Cycle No. 3 Compatibility Chart

Other Person's Number	GUIDE
1	Your energy and vitality, added to the leadership of the other person, makes this a vital combination. You can become builders of fame and fortune as well as happiness in your association. However, you should be careful not to attempt too many projects; concentrate on a single purpose together.
2	Research and literary work make good fields for you to enter together. You can contribute talent and magnetism to the combination, while the other person assumes the practical application of your ideas. Do not fluctuate in your attitude to retain balance here.
3	Like attracts like, and you and the other person will find each other attractive. You should succeed in learning from each other and carrying out educational plans. Success should also come from any enterprise dealing with the home or household affairs.
4	There may be friction here caused by your imaginative leanings and the earthy qualities of the other person. You would do well to listen and heed the other's advice, for it will no doubt be on a very practical plane. Avoid complaining. Combine your efforts

to be of help to others, and you will succeed in helping each other.

5 You should acquire great strength from the other person, for he or she can add the element of speed and the philosophy of "do it now" to your ideas. Think constructively, and don't fly off the handle. You can work successfully at the execution of projects of a humanitarian nature.

6 The word congenial well describes the potentialities of this relationship. The other adds balance to your rather playful tendencies. Give yourself the benefit of that influence, and you should both go far.

7 This association should lead to productive outlets for the talents of each of you. You will each stimulate the other, and your inventiveness and originality should flower into successful projects of advantage to you both.

8 The fulfillment of your highest hopes can come from this association if you will heed the advice of the other person. You can contribute your spunk and the other person the intellectual and financial genius needed for success in almost any venture. Follow; do not lead.

9 There may be a lot of talk and no results from this combination, unless you are willing to accept the foresight and the hunches that the other person contributes. For once, be the audience, not the star!

Your Life Cycle No. 4 Compatibility Chart

Other
Person's   GUIDE
Number

1
You provide a solid foundation to this relationship, and the other person contributes originality and initiative. This combination should be steadfast and permanent. You may occasionally be irritated by the leadership of the other person, but it is for your own good.

2
You will understand the other person, and will receive understanding, for your vibrations are compatible. There should be little competition and no friction between you. You bring out the best in the other person, and you receive perfect cooperation.

3
A splendid and lasting association can be formed between you and the other person if you will follow the other person's lead. The vibrations here add up to success in the fields of research, medicine, mysticism, and numerology. Exercise all your patience and tact.

4
A splendid combination for what the world calls "luck." This is really the result of two forces combining for financial success, power, and pleasure. Together, you can help the whole world with your plans, philanthropy, and good deeds.

5   You must act as the balance in this relationship, for the other person is likely to be talkative and flighty. Give ear, but see to it that your ideas are the ones that you carry out together. A mutual interest in occult matters or studies can help you both.

6   Help yourself to success by working with, not against, the other person. Together you can form a brilliant association wherein inventiveness and originality will lead to prominence and material gain, whereas each alone would remain a plodder on life's path.

7   Give the best of yourself to this relationship. Put in the hard work you are capable of, and let the other person contribute the children of his vivid imagination. The combination should produce splendid results. Mastery and power can come to both of you through mutual aid.

8   There should be fun and profit in this relationship. Understanding, sympathy, and a sense of humor possessed by both parties forecast excellent vibrations for a lasting and valuable association. Don't be extravagant.

9   You have the practicability which, added to the foresight of the other person, can make your friendship a real success. Listen, and learn. Add your workaday ideas to the imagination of the other person, and find success.

Your Life Cycle No. 5 Compatability Chart

Other
Person's
Number

GUIDE

---

1 Energy and vitality should mark this relationship, for you are both lively people and should get along well together. Speed and originality should mark everything you do together, and you should learn a lot from each other. Try to listen, and not do all the talking.

---

2 A lot can come from this partnership, or nothing at all. You will have to take the lead because the other person will be quiet, unassuming, and merely willing to listen and do as you say. Study together if you wish to advance. You must be interesting and directive.

---

3 You can do well at almost anything you try with the other person, for your vibrations add up to a success total. Monetary affairs, organizational work, and corporate affairs can be managed by the two of you if you work together. Your qualities complement each other.

---

4 You are sure to be attractive to the other person in this association because you probably possess all the traits that he or she lacks and needs. Give your speed to his practicability, and you should make a winning pair.

5 Temperamental outbursts could put a quick end to this combination, as you are both mercurial by nature. Each will have to restrain his talkative and flighty tendencies to get the real value out of this relationship, because it has the potentialities of being stimulating, original, and beneficial.

6 You should be very stimulating to the other person, for you have the qualities needed to bring about the display of the intellectual powers of the other person. Together, you form a fine union for the development of your intellectual powers and initiative.

7 You can get along with the other person only by restraining your natural verbosity. Be quiet to keep the respect and friendship of the naturally quiet other person. You can have a good time together when a good time is called for; otherwise, be rather serious.

8 You can profit much by association with the other person, for he or she will have the steadying influence and practical point of view that you may need. Follow the example he or she provides. Together, you can make almost any experience an adventure.

9 This relationship should bring out the best in you. Balance and foresight are provided by the other person, while you contribute an active mentality and personality. Wit and humor will be yours and vision will be provided by the other.

Your Life Cycle No. 6 Compatibility Chart

Other
Person's   GUIDE
Number

---

1   A very worthwhile association should grow between you, as you provide the serious side to the relationship and the other person provides the spark of originality needed. You should also be able to do the groundwork necessary to the success of mutual projects. Let the other lead.

---

2   This relationship spells success, for you can provide good ideas which the other person can work out successfully. Monetary ventures should succeed. Club and organization projects also augur well for both of you.

---

3   Perfect understanding should exist between you. You have many traits in common, but you probably are more quiet than the other person. As this may well be a lasting association, you should make long-range plans. Excellent for occult study, also.

---

4   New and creative projects should emanate from this relationship. You are both serious types, and together you can work out splendid plans. Collaboration should be a labor of love, as there should be no competition or friction between you.

5 This combination adds to a master number and purports powerful emanations from the relationship. You can contribute learning and experience while the other person adds the element of speed, intellectuality, and originality. Heed the advice you get from the other person.

6 Because you are both inclined to be serious by nature, this association should give you each a lot of pleasure. Together, each lightens the nature and temperament of the other. While your deeper moments are constructive, your lighter moments together can be very joyous.

7 There may be strong clashes between your personality and that of the other person, as your interests differ widely. You would each have to give in to the wishes of the other to a large extent to make a go of this association. Begin by building.

8 This might be a relationship that is all talk and no sincerity if you let it lapse from its high possibilities. Let the other person do the thinking and leading in your mutual projects; you can add the element of your greater deliberation, which acts like a brake.

9 Mutual understanding should make this a lasting friendship, partnership, marriage, or collaboration. Together you can go far, learn much, and improve each other's qualities.

Your Life Cycle No. 7 Compatibility Chart

Other Person's Number	GUIDE
1	This is a good combination for seeking the material profits and pleasures offered by life. Follow the lead of the other person; your function is to slow down the over-enthusiasm of the other person, and add to your ability to analyze things.
2	As you are both rather serene by nature, there will be little friction between you and the other person. Together you can successfully pursue the study of philosophy and occult subjects. Each of you will add to the placidity and peace of mind of the other.
3	Lots of activity will exist in this relationship. You will be the more quiet of the two, however, and take a back seat because you appreciate the more lively traits of the other person. Give your understanding, and accept the other person's contribution of energy.
4	In this association, you and the other person contribute vibratory powers which add up to a master number. A strong combination will result. You should get along well. You provide the ideas, and let the other person work them out.

5   You must be the ballast in the ship of friendship, for the other person may go off the course if you do not steer the ship. Keep calm at all times, even when you are exasperated at the talk and notions of the other person — if you want to stay friends.

6   Harmony does not exist here unless you are willing to take a back seat and let things ride. It would take a lot of hard work to make this combination a success, so decide how much effort you want to invest in it before you get too deeply involved.

7   Peaceful is the word to describe the association here formed. You are each adult in your point of view, and no arguments will take place as long as mutual respect exists between you. Writing and radio work would be an excellent project for you both to try.

8   You can give vision and sensibility to this combination while the other person gives executive ability and material and practical contributions. Give your quiet encouragement to the schemes and dreams of the other person, and you are both bound to go places.

9   Great depths of understanding and sympathy should exist between the parties of this association. Each has a subtlety of nature and inner understanding of universal laws that makes him or her a great person.

Your Life Cycle No. 8 Compatibility Chart.

Other
Person's
Number

GUIDE

1

You are both powerful and aggressive types, and will either get along splendidly or be deadly rivals. Together, you can each add to the other's splendor and courage; apart, you may annihilate each other. It is a matter of your choice.

2

You can make this a splendid association if you are interested enough to contribute your energy and vitality to the combination, for the other person can give only cooperation, not fire or brilliance.

3

Here is a combination with both parties full of life, magnetism, and strength of character. You should supplement each other, for you both have the same aims and ideals, and can help each other splendidly.

4

You each have traits in common that make for almost perfect understanding without even talking about your aims in life or what you might be seeking from each other. You have more power in your personality than the other person, and so you should be the leader in the partnership or friendship.

5   There is a lot of electricity loose in this vibratory combination. Lightning can strike very easily because you are both highly charged. If you want to get along with the other person, listen to his or her chatter, and restrain your own forces.

6   You can get inspiration and learning from this association, and it should prove of benefit to each of you. You express more power and magnetism, so be magnanimous, and don't overpower the other person with your strength.

7   In this combination, you are the fire, the heat, the force, while the other person is the light — cold, intellectual, but brilliant. You need the qualities of each other for a perfect union, so be diplomatic and tactful.

8   This can be a perfect union or a perfect revolution. You are both so powerful that you can extinguish each other. On the other hand, each of you can re-enforce the power of the other, and together, present a united front to the world.

9   Put some of your energy into this relationship, and you will soon see a mutually beneficial union arise from it. A splendid combination to do scientific, charitable, and philanthropic work.

Your Life Cycle No. 9 Compatibility Chart

Other
Person's   GUIDE
Number

---

1 This is a stimulating vibration for both parties. You can add inspiration to the combination while the other person contributes original ideas and inventive genius. Together, your work and play should shine with many facets of originality. Let the other person lead.

---

2 You will receive perfect cooperation from the other person. Your contribution to the relationship will be your sincerity, foresight, and vision. There should be no arguments or friction, as you each possess a serene nature.

---

3 Here the glitter of the other personality may seem almost too bright for you to bear unless there are other attractions to retain your interest. You do share a mutual understanding, and all is well as long as you do not try to be dominant.

---

4 You can make a marvelous team if you will be content to give your imaginative forces and brilliance to the earthy and practical contributions of the other party to this combination. You should form a fairly good balance, as you are inclined to heights, the other person to depths.

5   This will be a combination of speed and vision. Everything you share will take on the nature of flight through space, so you should try to take things in your stride if you want to continue this relationship.

6   You are both rather profound people. There should be no childish tricks, jealousy, or petty arguments between you. Each of you can give invaluable aid to the other and the result should be a magnificent partnership.

7   This is an almost perfect blending of vibrations. Each of you can help in the development of the heart, soul, and mind of the other. Tolerance, and mutual assistance should reign.

8   This is a case where you can gain much from the other person. You need the practical point of view he has to offer, and you can contribute your imagination and almost occult powers.

9   This is the kind of relationship considered to be carved out for you by destiny. Both of you are psychic, foresighted, and deep. A profound bond ties you together — for your mutual enlightenment.

Chapter XV
YOUR JOB

"Many are called, but few are chosen." You've probably used that phrase countless times in the past without pausing to think over what it really means. It has a definite significance that few people ever bother to try to fathom. About the only time people refer to one's "hearing a call" nowadays is when referring to the ministry. There, one still uses the expression, "He heard the call." It is because people hear the inner voice calling them to certain jobs or professions that they are known as their "calling."

Yet, it is still true that although many are called, few are chosen. You may hear the inner voice proclaiming that you should be an architect, or an actor, or a housewife, or almost anything that you *aren't!* You are not chosen simply because you are not living up to the possibilities of your own potentialities. You can only become what you want to be by: (1) knowing what you want to be, (2) having the capability to become what you want to be, (3) setting about to become what you want to be.

Numerology performs the function of suiting you to your proper calling by pointing out to you what your abilities are, what your career should be, and when to work to become what you want to be and what you are suited for.

Whether you are planning a career, are undecided about making a change, consult the numbers. Perhaps a friend wants advice; with the tables provided here, you can be of invaluable help. If you wonder whether you can qualify for a certain position, your birth date will answer your question.

You need not be a potential movie star, unhappy working in a factory. Nor need you be a potential wonderful craftsman being forced into a career as a concert pianist.

Follow the simple instructions given herewith to help you in successfully carving out your career.

How to Find Your Job Number

Job numerology functions according to your date of birth.

Add together the numerals of your date of birth. Then reduce the result to a single digit. The result is your Life Cycle Number; it is the same as your Job Number. For example, if you were born February 13, 1914, you put down the date in numerals, thus: 2 — 13 — 1914. Add all these together. Their sum is 21. Now add the numerals of the 21 together, thus: 2 plus 1 equals 3. This is your Job Number.

As these are only nine single digits, your Job Number will be one of the nine readings below. Read the one which applies to you for guidance in your career.

Appropriate Careers for Your Job Number 1

Actuary, ambassador, army officer, authorizer, buyer, captain, costume director, dance organizer, deacon, dean, discoverer, editor, export man, foreman, goldsmith, head of department, head of stock, house manager, jeweler, money lender, motion picture director, motion picture producer, president, principal, production manager, program director, radio station manager, sales manager, studio manager, tearoom manager.

Favorable days in any year to seek this type of employment or occupation, or promotion or adjustment in these career areas, are:

> January 9, 18, 27; February 8, 17, 26; March 7, 16, 25; April 6, 15, 24; May 5, 14, 23; June 13, 22; July 3, 12, 21, 30; August 2, 11, 29; September 1, 19, 28; October 9, 18, 27; November 8, 17, 26; December 7, 16, 25.

Appropriate Careers for Your Job Number 2

Agent, bank clerk, bond clerk, bell boy, boatswain, caterer, chain store clerk, chef, clerk, cook, engineer, export commission merchant, food industry in all its branches, hotel housekeeper, jobber, lawyer, operator, oyster farmer, porter, quartermaster, real estate agent, steward.

Favorable days in any year to seek this type of employment or occupation, or promotion or adjustment in these career areas, are:

> January 1, 10, 19, 28; February 9, 18, 27; March 8, 17, 26; April 7, 16, 25; May 6, 16, 24; June 5, 14, 23; July 4, 13, 22, 31; August 3, 12, 21, 30; September 2, 11, 20, 29; October 1, 10, 19, 28; November 9, 18, 27; December 8, 7, 26.

Appropriate Careers for Your Job Number 3

Administrator, chaplain, church administrator, civil service employee, community organizer, court clerk, corporation lawyer, curate, engineer, institutional administrator, judge, juror, justice of the peace, lawyer, magistrate, pastor, philosopher, playground director, play leader, politics, scout director, settlement worker, sportsman, Sunday School teacher, theatre manager, "trouble shooter," vocational school teacher.

Favorable days in any year to seek this type of employment or occupation, or promotion or adjustment in these career areas, are:

January 2, 11, 29; February 1, 19, 28; March 9, 18, 27; April 8, 17, 26; May 7, 16, 25; June 6, 15, 24; July 5, 14, 23; August 4, 13, 22; September 12, 21, 30; October 2, 11, 20; November 1, 10, 19, 28; December 9, 18, 27.

Appropriate Careers for Your Job Number 4

Architect, blue print expert, building trades in all branches, coal industry in all branches, cremator, engineer, industrial executive, farmer, financier, government official, lead industry in all branches, leather industry in all branches, mason, mine captain, mine draftsman, mine engineer, mine superintendent, minerologist, stone worker, superintendent of a public building, undertaker.

Favorable days in any year to seek this type of employment or occupation, or promotion or adjustment in these career areas, are:

January 3, 12, 21; February 2, 11, 20; March 1, 19, 28; April 9, 18, 27; May 8, 17, 26; June 7, 16, 25; July 7, 16, 25; August 5, 14, 23; September 4, 13, 22; October 3, 12, 21, 30; November 2, 11, 20, 29; December 1, 10, 19, 28.

Appropriate Careers for Your Job Number 5

Actor's agent, advertising agent, advertising copywriter, advertising salesman, all branches of aviation, author's representative, columnist, communications expert, consul, copy reader, copy writer, correspondent, courier, editor, editorial writer, feature writer, gag writer, graphologist, playwright, post office clerk, proof reader, publicity agent, publisher, public speaker, radio actor, rail road employee, reader, salesman, screen reporter, secretary, shipping clerk, sound engineer, trader, translator, writer.

Favorable days in any year to seek this type of employment or occupation, or promotion or adjustment in these career areas are:

> January 4, 12, 22; February 3, 12, 21; March 2, 11, 20, 29; April 1, 19, 28; May 9, 18, 27; June 8, 17, 26; July 7, 16, 25; August 6, 15, 24, September 5, 14, 23; October 4, 13, 22, 31; November 3, 12, 21, 30; December 2, 11, 20, 29.

Appropriate Careers for Your Job Number 6

Actor, airplane hostess, art director, artist, beautician, bridge instructor, call boy, cosmetician, drama coach, drama director, dressmaker, entertainment director, fair organizer, fashion expert, film industrialist, hair dresser, hostess, interior director, instructor, jeweler, make-up specialist, milliner, motion picture actor, musician, perfumer, policy writer, professor, property man, public festival director, scene painter, set director, singer, stylist, sugar industry — all brrnches, teacher, theatre manager, tutor, usher, wardrobe mistress.

Favorable days in any year to seek this type of employment or occupation, or promotion or adjustment in these career areas, are:

> January 5, 14, 23; February 4, 13, 22; March 3, 12, 21, 30; April 2, 11, 20, 29; May 1, 19, 28; June 9, 18, 27; July 8, 17, 26; August 7, 16, 25; September 6, 15, 24; October 5, 14, 23; November 4, 13, 22; December 3, 12, 21, 30.

Appropriate Careers for Your Job Number 7

Aerial navigator, arbitrator, archeologist, astrologer, civic leader, electrical engineer, healer, instrumentalist, inventor, investment analyst, jazz musician, laboratory research worker, labor mediator, lamp man, library cataloguer, mechanic, modern musician, photographer, psychic investigator, riveter, research specialist, scientist, transportation clerk.

Favorable days in any year to seek this type of employment or occupation, or promotion or adjustment in these career areas, are:

> January 6, 15, 24; February 5, 14, 23; March 4, 13, 22; April 3, 12, 21, 30; May 2, 11, 20, 29; June 1, 10, 19, 28; July 9, 18, 27; August 8, 17, 26; September 7, 16, 25; October 6, 15, 24; November 5, 14, 23; December 4, 13, 22, 31.

Appropriate Careers for Your Job Number 8

Acrobat, analytical chemist, armorer, army, banker, barber, broker, carpenter, cashier, charity worker, crime expert, dock worker, druggist, dynamiter, engineer, exterminator, financial expert, fire arms expert, fireman, foundry worker, iron worker, military expert, naval expert, philanthropist, philanthropical or charitable institute employee, prison attendant, steel worker.

Favorable days in any year to seek this type of employment or occupation, or promotion or adjustment in these career areas, are:

> January 7, 16, 25; February 6, 15, 24; March 5, 14, 23; April 4, 13, 22; May 5, 14, 23; June 2, 11, 20, 29; July 1, 10, 19, 28; August 9, 18, 27; September 8, 17, 26; October 7, 16, 25; November 6, 15, 24; December 5, 14, 23.

Appropriate Careers for Your Job Number 9

Axe man, butcher, clairvoyant, dentist, distiller, electrician, explorer, fisherman, hospital worker, hypnotist, logger, magician, manicurist, medium, metaphysical research expert, narcotics expert, occultist, organist, painter, philosopher, sailor, secret service agent, scientific research worker, surgeon, traveler, water expert.

Favorable days in any year to seek this type of employment or occupation, or promotion or adjustment in these career areas, are:

> January 8, 17, 26; February 7, 16, 25; March 6, 15, 24; April 5, 14, 23; May 4, 13, 22, 31; June 3, 12, 21, 30; July 2, 11, 20, 29; August 10, 19, 28; September 9, 18, 27; October 8, 17, 26; November 7, 16, 25; December 6, 15, 24.

WILSHIRE
Self-Improvement
LIBRARY

*The books listed above can be obtained from your book dealer
or directly from Wilshire Book Company. When ordering, please remit.
Send for our free 144 page illustrated catalog of self-improvement books.*

Wilshire Book Company
12015 Sherman Road, No. Hollywood, California 91605